MW00915493

A Long Road
To Christ

By Anthony B. Cook

Anthony B. Cook #163116
Southeast Correctional Center
300 E. Pedro Simmons Rd.
Charleston, MO 63834
or at www.AccessCorrections.com

ISBN: 978-1976172854
ISBN-10:1976172853

TABLE OF CONTENTS

DEDICATION & ACKNOWLEDGMENTS

This book is dedicated to the following people who've had a positive impact on my life. People who prayed for me, who supported me when I couldn't support myself, who never gave up on me. There are many more people out there or who have passed away, whose names I can't remember or never knew, but I want to thank them, also.

I want to thank Reading is Fundamental (RIF) for donating books to juvenile detention centers all across America. Those books helped me a great deal. There were times when I was so depressed and those books saved my life!

Here are a few names of the ones I do know who have had a positive influence in my life, in no particular order:

Ms. Grieger, Dr. Carrin, Hazel Franklin, my mother, Mrs. Chadwick, Mr. and Mrs. Crawford, Mr. & Mrs. Gray, Nan Hart, The Wigger's family, Kenny the truck driver, Mr. John Percinich, Vanita Hill, Mrs. Dent, Diane (my angel!), Preacher (miss you so much!), Natalie, Libby, Rebecca & Tim.

PREFACE

The man stood at the edge of the gangway, in the shadows, eyes daring all around. He had to be careful. He listened for unfamiliar sounds, sounds that didn't belong. There were none, just the distance bark of a dog. Reaching into the pocket of the old green Army jacket, he pulled out a cigarette, lit it and inhaled deeply. It was his first one in days, one he picked up off the ground an hour before. After finishing it, he left the gangway and walked into the darkness.

He had places to go, things to do. But first, he had to see someone. He had to see her. The winter wind cut through his thin shoes that he wore and his ears were getting cold. The snow had melted and turned into slush and it crunched with every step. He walked in the middle of the street, avoiding the sidewalk. All was quiet except for the dog barking up ahead, letting him know he was getting closer to his destination.

He had to see her, talk to her. He was in trouble and she'd know what to do. He hadn't seen her in years but he knew she'd be happy to see him. Stopping on the corner, he stood watching the big German shepherd across the street, straining against the chain around its neck, its canines exposed. The man sighed, walked across the street, squatted and petted the dog on its head.

The grass was soft and mushy under his feet as he neared her. She was there waiting, where she'd been for years, just waiting because she knew he would come. The man's heartbeat increased and tears began to flow as he kneeled before the tombstone, before her, and confessed.

CHAPTER 1

"But Jesus said, Suffer little children,
and forbid them not, to come unto me; for
of such is the kingdom of heaven." And
He laid his handle on them, and departed
thence." – Matt. 19:14-15

Even at age four, waking up home alone was nothing new to me, or for any other kid living in Kinloch, Missouri. The day started like others before, me not having a clue where my parents or siblings were. Even before getting out of bed, I knew I was alone in the house. If my siblings were there, I'd hear them even if I didn't see them because they'd be kicking up all kinds of ruckus.

I was tired. I didn't get much sleep because my mother had some of her friends over the night before. Loud and drunk friends. It wouldn't have been so bad if the bedroom I shared with my brothers had a door. I laid in bed staring at the ceiling, watching roaches running in and out of cracks. I was glad seeing them out, it meant the mice weren't. I was scared of them, something about their beady eyes gave me the creeps. I tried everything I could think of to keep then out, but nothing worked, they ate through everything!

Moving the covers aside, I sat up, looking around the room. There was an old wooden table with a lamp on top, and a dresser missing its doors. The window was boarded when we moved in, so I had to peep out the back door to see if any 'possums were out. People in Kinloch ate them, so there weren't many around. I didn't care how hungry I got, I wasn't eating nobody's 'possum!

When my feet touched the cold hard wood floor, it sent a chill throughout my body. I looked towards the closet for my jacket, but it wasn't hanging there, nor on the floor where I put it sometimes. It was a raggedy black jean jacket my mother bought at a thrift store. I think she pad a dollar for it. I walked to the kitchen looking for something to eat, but knew I wouldn't find anything We seldom had food at home, the only times we did was the first of each month, but after that we were done.

The cabinets and fridge were empty, so I walked back to the bedroom and put my shoes on. I'd slept in my clothes (a black t-shirt and worn Levi jeans), so I was good to go. I stepped outside to a cold early spring day. My jacket was laying across the rail of the wooden porch. I picked it up, shook it out, then put it on. My mother hug it on the rail sometimes because she didn't like the way it smelled.

I stood there a minute, looking up and down the street. Our two bedroom, one bath house sat on a long narrow street. There were 40 houses on it, but most were vacant. Sometimes, during the day, my brother Demetrice and I'd play hide and seek in them. My mother didn't mind until he fell through the floor and broke his leg. But even after that, we'd sneak in them. We just had to be careful not to get caught.

My stomach was growling while I stood considering my options. I had just two really – my grandfather's or the fire department. I had a friend who worked there named Pete. He was an old white man that always gave me something to eat whenever I was hungry. I didn't think he was a real fireman, but that's what he told me. I didn't care what he was, he was cool with me. Just the thought of us sitting on milk crates in front of the firehouse eating sandwiches, listen to his silly jokes, made me giggle out loud. Then my stomach growled even louder, settling the matter. To my grandfather's it was.

Mr. Leonard Crutcher was his name, drinking Rosie O'Grady was his game. That's all I really saw him do. That and get into fights with his landlord, Mr. Hicks. Mr. Hicks was the reason I had to _____ the fence surrounding the apartment complex. He had a berry tree in the back yard that Demetrice and I picked bone-dry, so whenever we came over, we had to be careful not to get caught. He'd ran me off with a mop stick the last time. I didn't know why eating berries was such a big deal. Way I figured it, if he didn't want nobody eating them, he shouldn't have planted the tree in the first place!

Mr. Hicks didn't like nobody and nobody liked him. Him and my grandfather got into a fight over a bottle of wine, and I sat in the tree watching the whole thing. They yelled at each other for a while, which I enjoyed, because as long as they were arguing I could eat berries. But then it got serious when he called my grandfather a "black grease monkey", sending him storming off to his apartment for a double-barreled shotgun. When he saw my grandfather coming, he pulled out an old handgun that had seen better days. Luckily, another drinking buddy of theirs broke it up before it got ugly.

With no signs of Mr. Hicks, I took off, running for my grandfather's apartment. When I made it, I twisted the door knob, stepped inside, and closed the door behind me. I stood there a moment, trying to catch my breath. I was in the living/dining   area but had a clear view of the whole apartment. It was small, only four rooms in all; kitchen, bathroom, bedroom and where I stood. I loved visiting my grandfather, and not because I could get something to eat, either. His apartment had carpet in every room except the kitchen, and I'd take my shoes off and walk around barefoot, or sit watching television on the recliner.

I locked the door and walked to his bedroom where I found him laying across the bed asleep. Turning, I went to the kitchen, fixed a peanut butter and jelly sandwich, then went back to his room. I sat on the leather couch, took a bite, and watched thoughtfully. I didn't know much about him, except what my mother told me. She said one time, when she was a child, he made her stand in the middle of the room with a lit Pall Mall cigarette in her mouth. Then he'd use a bullwhip to knock it out. That's the first horror story I ever heard!

He stood six foot tall, weighed 160 pounds, was dark skinned, and had long wavy black hair. She said he'd been in the Army and fought in the Korean War. I had the feeling he didn't care for me, not as he did my siblings. It's not that he'd treat me bad, it's just he never played with me like he would them. But one thing I did like about him was he kept money in his pocket and he'd give me a couple dollars to buy candy for me and my siblings.

He didn't like my father, and I heard him tell my mother many times she married a no good "so and so." I have only two memories of him myself. Him handing me a piece of candy, and cursing Pete out for giving me something to eat. The only thing I learned from my mother was he'd been to the Army, fought in Vietnam , became a drug addict, and "went crazy."

I sat in the recliner watching him, wishing I could move in. I didn't think he'd mind. The only problem would be Mr. Hicks and his stupid berry tree. The year was 1974, and we were living in the worst part of St. Louis at that time…Kinloch. Our neighborhood looked like a ghost town, it's alleys, a web of junkyards. Drugs were everywhere. Prostitution, people getting killed…I hated that place!

Kinloch, Missouri was predominantly black, with only three white people living there. The city wasn't small by any means, there were many buildings and houses. It's just most were vacant, or falling apart. The only buildings outside of the houses were a barber shop, funeral home, gas station, fire department, lounge and grocery store. Oh, and a police department that was closed down because the city had run out of money.

They couldn't afford to hire anybody so whenever we needed the police, we had to call Berkley, the next city over.

Everybody in Kinloch shared the same dream of moving out of there. Nobody liked the place. For some, their dream came true, but for most it didn't. They were the unlucky ones who got stuck in that hellhole and died, never knowing anything but disease, poverty and death. There were only three ways you died in Kinloch – old age, overdose or by a bullet. I saw people die in the most horrific ways imaginable. Sadly, some were kids I used to play with.

One day my mother came home with a new boyfriend on her arm. His name was George Wilson. He was a big guy, standing over six feet tall, brown skinned, had an afro and sideburns and weighed well over 250 pounds! she told us to pack our things in boxes because we were moving in with George in University City, Missouri. I didn't know how they took the news, but I was happy as I don't know what! I didn't have a clue where University City was and didn't care. All I cared about was getting the heck out of Kinloch. The only sad part was leaving my grandfather and Pete, my friend, behind.

So there we were, cruising down the street in George's station wagon, on our way to a better place. I was so happy, I rolled the window down and poked my head out. The scenery was amazing! The closer we got to our new home, the better the neighborhoods looked, and I couldn't believe how many white people I saw. They were all over the place! It was a long drive, and I enjoyed every minute of it. Eventually we turned onto a tree-lined street with beautiful houses on both sides. Halfway down the street, we pulled into the driveway of 1231 Purdue.

I heard a dog barking before we even got out of the car, and by the sound if it's bark, I could tell it was a big one. George saw the look of concern on our faces and told us the dog's name was Sabrah. She was a Doberman Pincher, and when we got out of the car she was trying to hop the backyard fence. I was scared to death! I never saw a dog that big. She was mostly black with small patches and had a small nub of a tail. She looked so mean to me, but George said she was friendly with everybody but the mailman. I found that funny, as George was a mailman himself!

When I first stepped into the house I remember thinking it looked like a space ship. I stood in awe at the living/dining room. All the furniture was new and it smelled like flowers. Turning to George, I asked what kind of house it was and he said it was a three bedroom, two bath ranch. I didn't know what a ranch was but the three bedroom, two bath thing I understood.

My brothers and I had a room, sister Tammy had one and George and my mother the other. Tim and I shared a bunkbed, while Demetrice had a twin bed sitting opposite ours. There was a large closet with more room than we'd ever need. The bedrooms were on the main level, along with the kitchen, bath, hallway and living/dining room. The finished basement had a laundry room, workshop, bath and another room where George had a buddy of his turn into a disco tech.

We settled in and a few days later, Demetrice and I was enrolled in U-Forest Elementary. It was the first school I attended, and honesty, I was scared. I snuck into a school in Kinloch and it had mice running around everywhere I looked. But U-Forest was different – neat, clean, food delicious and it didn't have mice. There were fifteen students in my class and I made friends with a couple of them but didn't get along with the rest.

One of my friends was a kid who lived across the street from us named Alex. For a five-year-old, he was pretty big, in good shape and played every sport imaginable. He was my only classmate who never made fun of me. Alex was cool, my teacher wasn't. I couldn't stand the sight of that old white woman! I was the only kid in a class who couldn't read or write, and I let her know the first day there. She was intolerant and had no patience whatsoever. She'd make me stand in the corner until my feet were sore, and if I complained or started crying, she whipped me. I heard the kids laugh every time, but Alex never did. He was so cool. My teacher wasn't.

If you lived in University City in the 1970's and early '80's, you were considered well off if you were black. There weren't many of us around at that time, mostly whites and Asians, and I saw lots of them where I went to the park. Heman Park was just a block from our house and I took Sabrah with me whenever I could. The park sat on over 25 acres. There was so much to do, you'd never get bored. There were merry-go-rounds, sand boxes, a skating rink, baseball fields and a basketball court. It even had a creek running through it. My brothers and I'd walk along side of it, trying to catch crawfish. My life in University City was going well until the fights started.

There were times George and my mother got along great, and times they got into the most heated fights. Fights that were one-sided because she'd hit him with everything but the kitchen sink. But he never laid a hand on her. My mother was an alcoholic and when drunk, lashed out at whoever was around at the time. Sometimes it was me and my brothers, but most of the time it was George who suffered her wrath. We were smarter than him, because when we saw her open a bottle of gin, we'd disappear. But he'd sit there as if he didn't know what was coming. George was such a good man and done nothing to deserve the pain he endured. I felt so sorry for him.

One night I woke up to the sound of my mother's voice. She was screaming at George about something. I lay in bed listening for a while, then tried going back to sleep. Finally I dozed off, but it wasn't long before I was woke up again. This time it wasn't her voice, it was her friend's Barbara Jean yelling, "Blow this mother f*%$#ing head off girl!" I knew what she was capable of doing. She lived in Kinloch and I though we left her there because I never saw her at our new home. I didn't know how she found her way to University City but knew she was dangerous as any man I'd known. I saw her stab and shoot people. Everybody in Kinloch was afraid of her.

I poked my head from under the cover, trying to see if my brothers were awake. It didn't look as if they were but I didn't know, wouldn't be the first time they'd faked me out. I saw George and my mother fight many times, but for some reason I sensed this was something else. I slid from under the cover, put my shoes on, then went to the bedroom door. I got in trouble before for walking around the house in the middle of the night so I tried to be as quiet as possible. I twisted the doorknob slowly, opened the door, and stepped into the hallway. The rest of the house was quiet but I heard Barbara barking in the backyard, which was never a good sign. I walked across the hallway to their bedroom and was frozen by what I saw.

It was the three of them, my mother, Barbara Jean and another woman I didn't recognize. They were standing around the bed yelling and screaming at a very tied-up George Wilson. My mother had one of his hunting rifles in her hands, pointed at his head. She pulled the trigger but he rifle jammed or she was too drunk to figure it out. I looked at George laying on the bed. They'd tied his wrists and ankles together with gray tape. He was crying, trying to say something, but couldn't because they'd stuff socks in his mouth. I turned, running from the room.

I ran to my bedroom but didn't get in bed. I ran to the closet, laid on the floor, curled into a ball and blacked out. When I woke, I heard only silence. I picked myself up off the floor and opened the door. The room was empty, and for a second I wondered where my brothers were at. I knew my mother wouldn't hurt them but wondered just the same. I thought about going to their bedroom but changed my mind. I saw dead bodies when we lived in Kinloch and had no desire to see more, especially George's.

I let the house and headed for school. I planned on telling my teacher what happened the night before, hoping she'd do something about it. When I got there, I went to class and told her what happened. Her reaction wasn't what I expected. She looked at me like I'd lost my mind. Then she went on, accusing me of making up the story to get attention. I couldn't believe what she was saying! Even as a child, I could have thought of better ways to get attention!

The next thing I knew, I was sitting on my bed with dried tears on my face. My mother had whipped me and was standing over me asking me why I told "them white people" what went on in our house? I found out George wasn't dead. The bad news were blackouts. I had them for as long as I could remember, and I sat there wondering, "How did I get home? How long was I out? What brought them on? Well, life in University City went on but George and my mother continued to fight. It got so bad I swear I didn't know if I could take another day of it.

CHAPTER 2: THE COBBANNE COURTS

"Therefore judge nothing before the time,
until the Lord come, who both will bring to
light the hidden things of darkness, and
will make manifest the counsels of the
hearts: and then they shall every man have praise
of God." – 1 Cor. 4:5

The most dangerous part of St. Louis during the 70's and early 80's was its westside. In any given year, half of all murders happened in that part of the city. The "Dirty West" it was called. But within the westside was a place even the people who lived on the westside didn't go. That place was a row of apartments one block long, and it was called "The Cabbanne Courts".

There were eight buildings, within each 12 apartments: six at ground level and six on the second floor. The buildings were identical except in color, and were shaped like a "U". Each "Court," as we called them, had a gangway leading to a small lot, and each lot to another Court. There was a parking lot running the length of the The Cabbanne Courts, separated by a sidewalk. That's where most of the drugs were sold. At night, or in broad daylight, it didn't matter. Not to the dealers.

Most of them were young men in the 20's and all carried guns. They didn't just have guns to protect them, they had the police. The police had been given two choices – work with the dealers, or against them. They tried against them but it didn't last very long. Rooting out crime in the Courts proved difficult, to say the least. There were many obstacles. The dealers posted lookouts on every corner, in every gangway, at the entrance of every Court, and on rooftops.

And then there was another problem – the back of the Courts. Running its length was a street named Hodimont. Some people called it "The Hodiment Tracks," but most referred to it simply as "The Tracks". It was a two-lane street where the Hodiment bus ran, and the only vehicles allowed on it were buses and police cars. Everybody in St. Louis new it, too, and therein lied the problem. The lookouts had a clear view of the whole street, and if a vehicle was spotted that wasn't a bus they knew it was the police.

The Cabbanne Courts were in the seventh precinct, and most of the district's police were cooked. The only time we'd see them was when they came to pick up bribes, or drop drugs off to the dealers. The department was just three blocks away but if you needed help and called them, it took an hour for them to show, if at all.

There were many different families living in the Courts but they all had two things in common. One, they were black. Two, they were on welfare. And nobody had a job, so I guess that makes three. The whole time we lived there I never saw anyone go to work. The people living there had two sources of income: welfare or drugs. When we lived in University City I heard my mother talking to her friends about The Cabbanne Courts, but I never thought in a million years we'd end up living there.

Eventually my mother and George broke up and we moved to a small apartment in north St. Louis city. The neighborhood was desolate, most of the houses were vacant, hardly nobody lived in it. I spent most of my time hanging out in the alley next to the apartment playing kickball with my brothers. Every day I'd sit in the upstairs window watching this old black man in the alley drinking wine and mumbling to himself. One day, when my brothers were off paying, I went down the alley and started throwing rocks at the dumpsters. I threw a big red brick at this one, not knowing the old man was asleep inside. He popped up like a Jack-in-the-Box and I almost had a heart attack when he came after me, chasing me down the alley with a rusty sword!

I don't remember going to school when we lived there but I do remember the shootings, day in and day out. I used to lay in bed, unable to sleep – it drove me nuts! My mother sent me to a mental hospital but I don't remember much, just them forcing me to take small orange pills that made me drowsy and pee a lot. It was so embarrassing, especially when it happened in my sleep.

My grandfather had been diagnosed with lung cancer and his condition got so bad he couldn't take care of himself. So my mother brought him to live with us. I remember watching him sitting in his wheelchair staring out the window at nothing, mumbling to himself. It was so sad. If nothing in life humbled my mother, it was her father's battle with cancer. I'm not saying she was a horrible person because she wasn't. We'd shared many good ties. It's just that when he came to stay with us, I'd never seen her love to that degree. She treated him so nice and with such respect.

I watched her sit with him all day long, holding his hand, speaking softly in his ear. She'd cry as he told her stories about her mother who died when she was just a child. The only thing she knew of her mother was the stories he'd share. His condition worsened and he was admitted to an assisted living facility specializing in treating/caring for cancer patients. We visited him several times, and with each visit we could tell he was getting worse. I loved the visits but not the facility. Even a blind man could see everybody there were old and dying. I never saw nothing like it. It even smelled like death.

The last time we visited him, it was raining and we were soaked when we entered the lobby. WE were met by an older white man who asked to speak to my mother in private. They walked to the side and talked. I don't know what about but whatever it was, it left her in tears. When they finished, she gathered us and we went to my grandfather's room.

The room was small, painted bright white and the only sound was the humming of the life support machine. My sister and brothers sat in chairs, my mother stood holding his hand and I sat on the bed next to him. He was wearing his favorite blue and white shirt but it was way too big for the frail of a man wearing it. I knew that day would be the last time I saw my grandfather.

Nobody said a word during the whole visit. What could we say? I think we all knew he was dying. My mother said it was time to go, then kissed him on his cheek and left the room, followed by my siblings. When I rose to get off the bed, he grabbed me by the arm, pulled me close to him, then let me go. I'll never forget that day. The way he looked, clothes he wore, the way he smelled. When we got back home, we filed out of the car and went into the house. When we stepped through the door the phone was ringing. I blurted out, "They're calling 'cause Granddaddy dead!" And he was.

There weren't many people at the funeral, most I didn't know, but there were a few familiar faces. Even old Mr. hicks had come to say his goodbye's. Barbara Jean was there, too, and I made sure I stayed as far away from her as possible. The only one there I was happy to see was George. I hadn't seen him for quite some time, and the first chance I got, I pulled him to the side and asked if I could come live with him. I told him my mother said were moving to a place called The Cabbanne Courts and I was scared because I heard it was worse than Kinloch. He said he'd loved to have me stay with him but he didn't want to go through the things he'd have to with my mother. The service ended, then we went to the cemetery and watched in silence as my grandfather's casket was lowered into the ground. After the funeral we went home, and my mother let with Barbara Jean to get something to drink. My sister and brothers went to watch television, I walked outside on the porch and watched the cars go by.

A couple weeks later, we moved to the Courts. Each Court had a name the white people who built it gave them, but nobody used them. The Court we moved into sat second from the corner, almost directly across the street from a park. The park's name was "Visitation." I don't remember why because nobody visited it. We learned our first day there when the Courts first opened several people got killed there, so everybody quit going there.

Our apartment was the first to the left on the second floor. We had to walk up two flights of wooden stairs to get to it. But I didn't mind, it was fun to me. Plus, it was daytime. The steps were inside the courtyard, and we learned the dope dealers hardly killed people there. They killed there when the sun went down. I remember times my friend Preacher and I would play on the steps, hear shooting, and wouldn't think about it. That was when we first moved in but things changed quickly.

I lived in many nasty, filthy, junky places but I'd never lived anywhere that could match the apartment we moved into. I heard the mice as soon as we stepped through the door, and could tell there were a gang of them. The living/dining room smelled of old we wood, and the paint on the walls were peeled almost bare. There were several holes in the ceiling that I learned to avoid like the plague. That's the first place I saw the mice. I kept my eyes glued on the ceiling, watching the holes. I could see their eyes in the darkness. They were watching me.

The kitchen wasn't much. It was small with a few appliances that looked like they were tired of being used. Off the living/dining room was a short hallway that led to the bedrooms. Halfway down the hallway was a closet with a furnace in it. I stopped in front of it on my way to the bedrooms and could hear the furnace roaring inside. I could hear the mice, too. They were in there. I looked up at the ceiling and there was a hole in it. I saw their eyes in the darkness. They were watching me.

There were three bedrooms at the end of the hallway. My brothers and I shared one, Tammy had one to herself and my mother took the other one. Every bedroom looked alike and were missing their doors. The windows were boarded and stayed that way until we moved out. The walls were painted bright blue, and had holes in them. I stared at the holes. I could see their eyes in the darkness. They were there. They were watching me.

We settled in and my mother began a relationship with a guy named Daryl Minner. He was in his early 30s, had a head full of hair worn in a perm, was slim, light skinned, and had an open-faced gold tooth. I didn't like him at all because he was a scandalous dope dealer who brought nothing but trouble into our house. But he did have a BB gun he let me use to shoot the mice with. Sometimes, when it wasn't a school night, I'd sit on the couch in the living room, waiting on them to come out. I was going to kill as many as I could, but they never showed their faces. I never saw one of them on those nights, but I sensed them. They were there. They were watching me.

I spent most of my time horsing around with a kid named Preacher. He was a year younger than me, eleven-years-old. He was skinny, dark skinned and everybody loved him. He was the most mild, carefree person I knew. And like so many other kids our age who worried about getting killed, he never did. We watched a couple get mowed down in the street. I remember seeing one kid get shot 17 times and then was run over by a car. Preacher was there that day and that was the only time I saw him cry.

He was the only kid in the Courts who wasn't afraid of mice. I was scared to death of them! There were days we'd be playing baseball in front of the apartments and I'd sense their presence. There were a couple of times I saw the curtains move. I couldn't see their beady eyes but I knew they were there. They were watching me.

Oh my God, I was scared! Huddled in the closet, listening to the gunshots. I was hot, sweating, and could feel the heat from the furnace burning the back of my neck. My chest was hurting and I could hardly breathe. I wrapped my arms around my legs, pulling them close to my chest. I didn't know who the people in our house were but knew why they were there. They were there to kill Daryl and anybody else who was there. That's the way they did it if you took a dopeman's drugs and he didn't pay on time; you were as good as dead. It didn't matter if you were a day late or a dollar short, they'd kill you.

I was crying for my mother so I put my hands over my mouth trying to stifle the sound. I kept my eyes glued to the bottom of the door, my heart skipping a beat every time a shadow passed by. I kept thinking the door would bust open and I'd be shot to rags. I didn't want to die. I put my head between my legs and looked down at the floor and saw a dozen baby mice staring up at me. They were huddled together, shaking. They didn't want to die, either. It's strange, when I look back at it now, how I used to be so scared of them. But that day I sat back in the closet, comforted by them. I whispered, "I'm sorry" then blacked out.

The shooting had stopped when I came to but I stayed where I was until the police got there. I heard their walkie talkies, so I yelled out to them to let them know where I was. You had to be careful in those days because they shot first then asked questions later, if at all. They pulled me out of the closet and questioned me, wanting to know if I saw the gunmen's faces. I was pretty shook up so I don't remember what I told them, if anything at all.

I was the only one home that day because I had a cold and was too sick to go to school. When I got up that morning my sister and brothers had already left for school and I didn't know where Daryl and my mother were. So I just rolled over and went back to sleep. I woke up to the sound of the front door being kicked off its hinges. Preacher and I had seen that happen to people in the Courts before, so I knew what it meant and that's why I jumped out of bed and ran for the closet.

The police asked the neighbors downstairs to look after me until my mother got home. I walked into their apartment, sat down on the couch, my hands clasped together. I couldn't get the images out of my head, all the bullet holes I saw when I walked out of the closet. I sat and wondered how long it would be before I got shot down like my good friend Preacher.

That was the saddest day, not just for me but for everybody in the Courts. Everybody loved Preacher. It didn't matter how sad you were, or what you were going through, he came around and we forgot about it. He was just that kind of person…and one day, he was gone forever. I was with him that day. We were throwing a baseball back and forth. I missed a catch and it rolled into the street. I started after it but he yelled he would get it himself. He ran, picked it up and that's when the shooting started. I dived behind a parked car and when I raised my head, I saw him fall face forward onto the concrete. His clothes bloody. The guy's wo were shooting at each other, saw what they'd done and then ran off.

Now, there I sat on the couch, wondering how long I had to live. Preacher was the fourth child gunned down in the Courts in a period of 13 months. No one survived, they all died. I sat there thinking about that. I thought about the neighbor who's couch I was sitting on. Her daughter was one of those children. Just thinking about that made me start crying again. She came over, sat on the couch and put her arms around me.

One day I was on my way to school but first wanted to stop by the apartment building across from Visitation Park. There was an old black woman who sold candy to kids in the Courts out of her house. I had some change I got for washing one of the dopeman's cars and planned on buying candy to take to school. I always walked in the middle of the streets because I was afraid someone could be hiding behind a car, ready to jump out at me. It was a quiet morning without many people out and about. There were two men coming my way, one on either side of the street. I watched them looking back and forth at each other as they got close to where I was crossing the street. I didn't see or hear the first shot, but felt a bullet slam into my chest. My ears started ringing as I fell to the ground and my chest started burning. I called out for my mother but could hardly breathe. Then one of them came and stood over me with a gun, raised it, and pumped two more bullets into my chest. I felt a warmness spread over my body, then the darkness.

I woke up a couple months later to a quiet hospital room. In the corner was a wooden table with a vase of flowers on top of it. I laid there a minute, listening to the silence. There wasn't much physical pain but I was so tired and sick inside. I remember thing, "Why can't I just die?" It would be years later before I got an answer to that question.

People were saying I had been an innocent victim of 'random gun violence' but I don't know. I think they wanted to kill Daryl, but couldn't get him, and figured they'd hurt him by killing one of his family members. I don't know for sure, to be honest, but I'll ask the mice the next time I see them. They witnessed the whole thing.

CHAPTER 3: DIANE

"And there appeared an angel unto
him from heaven, strengthening him." – Luke 22:43

"Gotta find me an angel in my life…" Aretha Franklin's song playing on the radio as my mother cleaned the living room carpet. I stood in the doorway watching her with a broom and a bucket of bleach water. That's how it was done in the ghetto. Couldn't' afford an angel, either. I didn't even know what an angel was. I'd seen the little fat white babies on the television with wings, but who knew of they were real?

I turned and walked out of the house, on my way to the back yard. There was something I needed to get before I hit the alleys. I hid my slingshot under an old pile of wooden boards. It wasn't a real one, not the kind you'd buy from the store, but it was okay I guess. I made it out of three small branches I'd torn off the neighbor's tree, a rubber band and a square piece of cardboard. I loved putting rocks in it and shooting them at dumpsters, and other times I'd sent them sailing through the air just to see how far they'd go. That's how I broke the neighbor's window.

I picked the slingshot up then headed for the alley. I wanted to turn left and go towards Union Boulevard but then I'd have to be lucky and catch this German Shepard asleep. He was in a back yard that didn't have a fence around it and if I wasn't careful, he'd see me and come running. Every time he got after me, I had to hop on top of one of the dumpsters until he got tired of barking at me and left. But even then, I had to be careful because he got hip to what I was doing. A couple of times he hid behind the garage and tried to sneak attack me when I got down. Well, I only thought about going left for a few seconds, that's all the time I needed to make up my mind – I was going right.

Going right wasn't as bad as left because there weren't dogs that I'd have to deal with. But there was a girl I saw all the time when I went that way, sitting on her back porch reading books. I didn't like seeing her there. She lived there, so I

15

guess she had a right to do whatever she wanted. I didn't care if she sat there until her eyeballs went dry, I just didn't like the way she looked and smiled at me when I walked by. That got on my nerves!

I'll admit, sometimes I liked it. Her name was Diane. I know because she told me so the day she invited me to sit on the porch with her. I was enrolled in school but hardly went; and when I didn't, I'd walk the alley's all day. I only went to school for two months but stopped going because my teacher told me I was a slow learner and had a behavior disorder. The principal and the teacher talked my mother into sending me back to the mental institution that specialized in "healing" mentally ill children. What made it so bad was I didn't know what was going on. When my mother was driving towards south St. Louis, I had no idea that twenty minutes later I'd be wrestling with a bundh of white people trying to stick a needle in my arm. The last thing I remember was laying on the ground and hearing my mother's voice, "It's for your own good baby…"

I stood watching Diane for a second. I never thought she'd ask me to sit on the porch with her. I walked over, sat down, and outside of giving my life to Jesus years later, it was the best decision I've made in my whole life. She started talking and I started sweating. She asked me why I didn't go to school and I told her the problems I was having with the other kids and my teacher. I also told her I was taking medication and the effect it was having on me. She asked me why I was on medication and I told her cause I was crazy. She said I wasn't crazy and should stop taking the medication. The she asked if I wanted her to teach me how to read and write.

We spent the whole summer on her back porch with books spread all over the place. She was so kind to me, even letting me play with her hair. Sometimes she took me walking throughout the city and we'd go through neighborhoods I was to go through myself. Whenever we were together, I didn't fear anything. We rode the city buses and she taught me how to read the maps and schedules. She took me to Forest Park and we visited the zoo, art gallery, went fishing, went to the science center, where I learned what a star was.

The best part was riding the train that ran through the zoo, when she'd point to the animals, tell me what they were and what country they were from. I really loved when she held my hand, read to me, or asked my opinion about something. That's where she messed up because I'd talk her ears off! Diane had a way of teaching me things no one else could, or would. She never cursed or yelled at me when I made a mistake. She told me she was going to go to college to be a school teacher and I told her she didn't need to go to college to be something she already was to me. I made sure she promised to visit during vacations, too. That was the last thing I said to her, and the last time I saw her alive.

At the end of August I was in bed asleep when my brother Demetrice woke me saying Diane's house was on fire. I told him to stop playing with me. He always did that, telling me something that happened to her because he knew how much I cared about her. I rolled over to go back to sleep and he shook me again and swore he wasn't playing. I looked into his eyes and could tell he was serious. I hopped out of bed, ran down the steps and out the front door to a street full of police cars, fire trucks and ambulances.

The neighbors were crowded on the sidewalks and in front of the street. I looked towards Diane's house and saw flames shooting from the windows and front door. I ran down the street but a fireman grabbed me and carried me to my mother. In her arms, I watched as the fire took the life of the only friend I had. When the fire was out, I watched in horror as they carried Diane's burnt remains out of the house. I had never known such pain.

CHAPTER 4: 4763 NORTHLAND

"But that we write unto them, that they
abstain from pollutions of idols, and from
fornication, and from things strangled,
and from blood." – Acts 15:20

When I was thirteen-years-old, we moved to 4763 Northland. The new house was an all brick, white one story with four bedrooms, two bathrooms and a fenced backyard. The first thing I noticed when we drove up to it was the huge porch and I remember thinking it would be a cool place to hang out. There were three bedrooms on the main level and one in the basement. My mother was dating a guy named James Haynes so they had a room, my sister Tammy had one but the third bedroom on the main level was so messed up it wasn't safe to sleep in. Demetrice, Tim and I slept in a huge open space. I wasn't upset about that at all, because there were plenty of mice down there. I heard them when I first went down to the basement. I didn't see them but I knew they were there and was so glad they were watching me.

The backyard was had a carport with a dog house on it and I don't know where my mother got this fluffy little collie but she named him Tony, after me. He was black and white and had energy to spare. Tony didn't like other dogs and would fight them at the drop of a hat. We tried keeping him in the yard but he always found a way out. We scratched our heads for months, trying to figure out how he did it, and then we caught him. Come to find out he'd dug a hole under the fence and when he left, we drug a flat board over it.

James and I didn't like each other. I didn't like him because he always got drunk, then tried to tell me what to do. I'd let him know, every chance I got, he wasn't my real father. He was a tall, slim, dark skinned man and wore his hair in a perm. Kind of put you in the mind of a skinny James Brown. He had an old Chevy truck that wouldn't start most of the time. But when it did, he'd take me with him on jobs he did in the white people's neighborhoods. I learned a lot from him, such as how to tuckpoint, cut grass, paint and much more.

When we were on job sites I'd walk through those white people's houses and trip off on how big they were. They had swimming pools, tennis courts – all kinds of things. I'd never seen anything like it! I even thought about stealing something that I could sell to buy new clothes, but was scared because they might have had cameras. James never let me see how much money he was paid. I always had to go outside or wait in the truck. He thought he was being slick but I new what that jive turkey was doing. He never gave me more than five dollars, even though I did most of the work.

Sometimes when we were on a job, white people would come out and talk to us. I listened to them complain about not being able to decide if they'd vacation in California or New York. I thought they were crazy, at the very least, just different. Who'd complain about something like that? I'd been happy complaining about Adidas or Converse! Some of them owned businesses and I listened to them talk to James about them. I even snuck in their libraries and read their books and magazines, dreaming of owning my own business someday. We still lived off welfare so we weren't starving but we didn't eat like them white people ate! They asked me all the time if I was hungry and I always said no.

Rev's was where I had my first fight. I was playing Pac Man with this kid, Marlo, who got mad because I was beating the brakes off him. I was the best player in our neighborhood but sometimes I let people win a few games, then bet a dollar or two and beat them easily. It happened on a Saturday, the store was packed with kids but none of them helped me fight Marlo. They were scared of him and I was, too. I don't know what I was thinking of, trying to con him.

Marlo was a big bully that went around our neighborhood punking everybody. Like I said, they were scared of him and I was, too. But the difference between them and me was I wasn't afraid to fight. I wanted to fight him, even though I knew I couldn't whip him. I used to see him walking up Northland every day, checking me out. The first couple of times he did that, we'd stared each other down until he passed my house. But that wasn't why I wanted to fight him. It was because it sucked that he stole my bicycle I got for Christmas!

I didn't catch him in the act but knew he'd done it because he was walking our alley one day and saw where I'd hid it behind the dog house. I woke up the next morning and it was gone. I went looking for him but didn't know where he lived. He stayed out of sight for a week or so but I knew eventually he'd show his face. He had to because bullies didn't pick on people unless someone's there to watch.

The thing about it was I knew whenever I ran into him, I'd get my tail whipped real good. So I figured if I was going down, I was going down swinging AND with some money in my pocket. My mother gave us five dollars on welfare day and I planned on using mine to bait Marlo and take his money. After a week of not seeing him, he popped up one day, walking up Northland with his boys. I was standing on the porch listening to a Michael Jackson album on my boombox. We didn't say anything to each other but he did give me the mean mug. The following day I went to Rev's with my five dollars. When I walked in, Marlo was posted up in the corner with his boys around him. I walked to the video game, acting like I didn't see him.

My heart was pumping so hard, I thought it would bust out of my chest but I knew I had to go through with my plan because if I didn't, I'd be labeled a punk or a sissy. By this time, everybody had heard what he'd done and I had to do something about it. I didn't tell Demetrice about it when it happened because I knew he'd go after Marlo. He was Marlo's age and could have easily whipped him but if that happened, people would still think I was a punk. I kept my mouth shut but somebody told him about it and he said he was going to kick Marlo's butt 'on sight.' But I explained to him that if he did that, what about the next bully? And the next? I wanted to do it, not for somebody else but for myself.

I felt Marlo standing behind me, watching me lose a couple of dollars, and knew it wouldn't be long. I bet a kid fifty cents a game and let them beat me. Marlo was big and strong and I'd braced myself for the sucker punch but it didn't come. Instead, he offered to bet me ten dollars for every game I put up and I bet the three dollars I had left. If I lost, I lost three dollars. But if I won, I'd be thirty dollars richer.

I didn't just beat him, I talked crazy to him the whole time. I had everybody laughing at him, including his boys. And that's where I tripped. I didn't just trip, I learned a lesson: "don't talk, swing". I talked and Marlo swung. He hit me so hard, I saw Jesus!

After that day, it was on like Donkey Kong! Every time I saw him, I was swinging, trying to knock his head off. And every time, he kicked my tail. And eventually he got tired of me and sent word he was through. So we called a truce and that was the end of that. I was cool with that because I'd gained the respect of kids my age but what I really wanted was the respect of the older guys in the neighborhood. I knew I couldn't get it my fighting, I had to get some money because that was the only thing they respected. You could beat up or kill a thousand people but if you were broke, it wouldn't mean a thing on the streets of St. Louis.

I had an old BB gun hid in the basement and figured I'd use it to rob somebody. I laid in bed sweating and nervous about it. I'd never robbed nobody before but had a good idea how because I saw it plenty of times when we lived in the Courts. I also saw people get killed trying to do it. I saw this one guy pull a sawed off shotgun on a dope dealer and say, "This is a robbery, don't make it a murder." The dope dealer reached into his jacket and pulled out a pistol and blew the guy's head off.

If I was faced with the same situation like that would-be robber was, I didn't have the heart to pull the trigger. That's what I was worried about. Plus, I didn't have a real gun. There were plenty of people around that I could rob but they all knew me and where I lived. I thought about going to the white people's neighborhood and rob one of them but it was too far to walk. Marlo had stuck to his story that he hadn't stole my bicycle but I knew that negro was lying.

I got out of bed and walked to the furnace on the far side of the basement. I'd cut a small square out of an old blanket and made a small bed for the mice. When we first moved in they wouldn't come out when I called so I made the mice bed and put food on it. I'd sit up half the night waiting on them to come out, but they wouldn't until I fell asleep. It took some time and a whole lot of hamburger meat but eventually they came. First it was just two of them and I named them Tom and Jerry, but by the end of the month it was a gang of them. I tried giving each a name but it was too hard telling them apart. I gave up and settled on 'The Brady Bunch.'

The BB gun was hid in a hole in the wall, the same hole The Brady Bunch came in and out of. When I first hid it there I felt kind of bad, didn't seem right to me. I gave them a call but they didn't come, so I called again. Still no Brady Bunch. I reached in the hole and except for the BB gun it was empty. I was worried because they were always there, if not for just a few of them. I ran and grabbed a flashlight, then used it to see further into the hole. They were gone. I turned the flashlight off and sat with my back against the wall, wondering what had happened to them. Whatever I did, I knew they were gone.

I was enrolled in Hicky Middle School after summer, and started sixth grade. My teacher was a middle-aged black woman name Ms. Grant. She was nearly six feet tall, slim, brown skinned and wore her hair in a perm. She never said much to her students, just gave us assignments and tell us to do them. Most of us didn't do a lick of schoolwork the whole semester and she still passed us on to seventh grade. There were twelve students in my classroom, including myself I was cool with only one of them, a kid named Carlos Spann.

He was the tallest and oldest student in our class, I think sixteen-years-old. He'd flunked fifth grade at least twice, that I know of. But he was a good kid, just couldn't keep his hands off other people's girlfriends and that's how I met him. I was in the liquor store buying candy a couple of days before school started and another kid named Nathan Blue was getting ready to beat him down because Carlos had blew a kiss at his girlfriend. Carlos liked to say he was a lover, not a fighter. I don't know about the lover part but knew he couldn't fight a lick.

When I walked out of the store, Nathan had him up against the wall, smacking him upside the head. I grabbed Nathan and slung him to the ground. I never liked Nathan because he was just like Marlo, a big bully picking fights with people he knew he could beat. But the thing of it was he wasn't a very good fighter and only won because nobody would fight back.

Nathan got off the ground and came up swinging, trying to hit me in my face. I grabbed him again and slung him back to the ground. This time, when he got up, he didn't swing at me. He looked down at the outfit he was wearing, then walked away. I turned to Carlos, asking if he was okay and if he wanted me to walk him home. He said it was cool, then started walking up St. Louis Avenue towards his house. I stayed on the sidewalk watching him until he turned the corner, then picked up my bag of candy and headed home.

I don't know why I kept messing with Carlos. He wasn't a bad kid, it's just that every time we were together, I ended up fighting somebody over something he'd done. Girls. That's all he knew. He was a handsome kid, light skinned, tall, green eyes, jerry curl and the best break dancer in school. He lived on Terry avenue, a couple blocks over form us so that day at the liquor store wasn't the first time I'd seen him. And despite all the crap I went through being his friend, all the times I got my tail whipped over something he'd done, I'll never regret being his friend.

The year was 1984, the year of Michael Jackson, Michael Jordan, rap music and jerry curls. Everybody wanted to be like Mike, dance like Mike, look like Mike an dress like Mike – including me. My mother was still on welfare but had broke up with James so there wasn't much money coming in. She did everything she could keeping us in clothes and fed. Somebody once told me, "There's no greater love than that of a mother." I didn't see that then but it's so easy to see it now. How I wish I'd known what I know now, how much pain I put her through.

I had one pair of pants, three shirts and a pair of Converse to my name. I spent most days watching MTV though I really don't know why, because all they showed was a bunch of light skinned, jerry curl wearing negros. They had all the cars, all the women and I couldn't stand those negros. But still, I wanted to be like them. I hardly looked in the mirror because I knew I wouldn't like what I'd see. My black face. I couldn't stand the sight of it.

I tried using Noxzema to lighten my face but it didn't work. I stole a jerry curl from National supermarket but when I put it in, it burned my scalp. What I really wanted was a girlfriend. Every boy at school had one and that was because the girls didn't find me attractive. I wasn't attractive to them because I had no money, no jerry curl plus I was dark skinned. I couldn't do anything about my skin complexion or the jerry curl but I could do something about the money. That was all I needed anyway. And if I got my hands on enough of it, I could buy any girl at school I wanted.

CHAPTER 5: 'LIL COOK

"He that trusteth in his riches shall fail;
but the righteous shall flourish as a branch." – Prov. 11:28

"Why do you keep running away from home Anthony? Why did you steal the car? Were you joy riding or planning to strip it down and sell the parts? Are you on drugs, Anthony?" The detectives were questioning me for what seemed like hours. I was sitting in the city juvenile detention center, in big trouble, being questioned like I tried to kill the president.

I hated the way I looked and every time I looked in the mirror, I hated what I saw. I saw an ugly dark skinned nappy headed nigga. That's what I saw and was thinking the day I tried to end it all. I went to the bathroom, closed the lid on the toilet and sat down. I thought about what I'd overheard the girls at school saying about me. I was too dark skinned to be their boyfriend. I put my head down and noticed my jeans were wet. I was crying.

James kept a straight razor in the cabinet. I got up, picked it up, then sat back down on the toilet lid. I rolled up my shirt sleeve and cut my wrist. The blood didn't shoot out like I thought it would so I cut it again and started to panic because I knew if I didn't hurry my mother would come looking for me. I grabbed a towel and whipped where I'd cut myself, trying to figure out why I wasn't bleeding to death like the people on the television.

I wiped the razor and saw the rust. It was too rusty to cut my wrist but did have a point on it so I stood, took off my t-shirt and plunged it into my stomach. The pain was so bad I almost fell to the floor. I dragged it across my stomach but the sight of my innards scared me and my legs gave out from under me. I wanted to call my mother but it got dark. When I woke up I was laying in a hospital bed at Barnes Hospital. My mother was sitting beside the bed crying saying, "Jesus" over and over again. She looked at me and rubbed my face. I couldn't think of anything to say but, "I'm sorry momma."

When I was released from the hospital, we drove home in silence. When we pulled in front of our house, it seemed the whole neighborhood was out. I didn't want to get out in front of them but had no choice. I got out and looked around. Everybody I looked at averted their eyes. They were afraid of me but not as afraid as they would be in the months and years ahead.

There were only two ways to get respect in my neighborhood. Money and fear. I wanted both, and made up my mind I didn't care how many heads I had to crack or necks I had to break, I was getting both. I knew I couldn't get what or where I want to be, looking the way I did. I had to change. I had to get my hands on some money.

There was a drug dealer who lived down the street from us named Thomas Lathan, but everybody called him by his nickname, Tommy Red. He was a light skinned black guy, wore a jerry curl and was in his early twenties. He owned several cars, wore lots of jewelry, had money and the girls. I thought he had a real cool nickname and racked my brain trying to figure out one for myself that was as cool as his. I settled on 'Lil Cook. Now all that was left was getting some money. That was the key to everything, you could get anything you wanted with it.

Tommy Red had so many cars he couldn't park all of them in front of his house so he had Randy Valentine park some in front of his house on Couples Avenue. When we first moved to Northland I got around the neighborhood on my bike or walking. I never liked walking on sidewalks and the only time I did so was when I was with Diane. But seeing Tommy Red's cars and the girls hanging out in the front of his house changed all of that. I still walked the alleys but made it a point to pass his house on my way to school or the arcade.

Tommy Red was what we called 'nigga rich' and he wore enough jewelry to tie a dog in the yard. Every time I passed his house, he was out in front selling drugs and I'd wonder why the eighth district police never bothered him or anybody working for him. Come to find out, he'd bribed every police in our neighborhood, including detective Clyde, who a year later he paid to kill me.

On welfare day, Tommy Red would have a line of cars in front of his house, stretching around the corner to Nate's barbershop. One of the kids he had on his crew was Tracie Shelton, who went by the name KC. KC sold drugs and was the best car thief in our neighborhood. He spoke to me from time to time and that made me feel good because the other kids who were making money were stuck-up, acting like their dookie didn't stink.

25

I wanted to get nigga rich but not by selling drugs because I'd seen too many people get shot and killed over that junk. I didn't know how to steal cars but I figured I could learn easy enough. KC was the key. He'd spoke to me but wouldn't be caught dead with nobody who didn't dress as cool as he did. The only people he'd let in his inner circle were people with money or at least they looked like they had some.

I woke the following morning with stealing clothes on my mind. There weren't any department stores in our neighborhood so on welfare day, my mother took us shopping in the white people's neighborhood in south St. Louis. I didn't have money for bus fare but did have a bicycle Demetrice gave me, seeing that punk Marlo didn't own up to stealing mine and giving it back. South St. Louis was a long way off, even with a bicycle, and I didn't know if I had enough energy to make it that far – but I was going to try!

I peddled up Kings Highway for I don't know how long and by the time I got to the south side, my whole body was sore. I was going to Ventures because I knew the white people wouldn't follow me around the store like they would at a famous bar. Another reason was because if I got chased out of there, it would be easier to get away.

I hid my bicycle in a garage a block away from the store, hoping it wouldn't get stolen. Somebody told me white people didn't steal bicycles and I was hoping that was true, because if it wasn't, I'd have a long walk back to north St. Louis. I'd been to Ventures plenty of times, so I knew where to find what I was looking for. I walked directly to the jeans section, grabbed a pair that were my size, then did the same thing in the shirt and shoe sections. I took them to the dressing room, took my clothes off and exchanged them out with the new ones. I put the clothes I'd worn there in a plastic bag and then tossed it into the trash on my way out of the store.

After the detectives finished questioning me, I was put in a holding cell. It was cold, had a steel toilet and sink, with a steel slab attached to the back wall for a bed. The detectives said I wouldn't get a mattress until I was processed in. A couple of kids told me if your parents didn't pick you up, you'd get processed in and took upstairs to one of the units there. I sat on the steel slab wondering what I was going to tell my mother. Then my mind drifted back.

I was tired as heck by the time I made it back to the northside, but not so tired that I'd miss the meeting with KC. I really wanted to hook up with Tommy Red but the only way that would happen was through KC. When we did meet, I asked if I could get in on stealing cars with him. He asked why and if I knew how to drive. I told him I wanted to be a nigga rich like him and Tommy Red and I didn't know how to drive but I was willing to learn if he'd teach me. He said if I wanted to make the kind of money him and Tommy Red did, I had to sell drugs but I let him know that wasn't happening.

We put my bicycle in the trunk of his car, drove to Lambert Airport and stole a car off the parking lot. KC drove it to another parking lot and taught me how to drive. I found that it wasn't that hard to do. The hardest part was driving it back to the airport to pick his car up from the lot. Didn't make sense to me because I thought it would have been smarter if we caught the bus. What if we got pulled over? After picking up his car, we drove to a vacant garage and stripped it down. I didn't know what he did with the parts and I didn't care. All I cared about was the hundred dollars he gave me for helping him steal the car. I had big plans! I was going to use the money to buy new clothes, get some girls and get a jerry curl.

We hooked back up later that day, was riding around and drinking, when the police pulled us over. We hopped out and ran. Now there I was, sitting in the detention center, wondering how I got caught and he didn't. I could've sworn I saw him get tackled by one of the police officers like I did. I asked the detective about that and he said KC got away. But how?

CHAPTER 6: VANITY

"For the earnest expectation of the
creature waiteth for manifestation
of the sons of God. For the creature
was made subject to vanity, not willingly,
but by reason of him who hath subjected
the same in hope." - Rom. 8:19-20

I became the most popular student at Hickey Middle School, and enjoyed every minute of fame. I had new clothes, money and a girlfriend. I was cheating on her but she didn't care, as long as I took care of her. I drove a different stolen car to school almost everyday of the week. When I first started stealing cars, we'd strip them down and sell the parts, but went to selling the whole car to mafia dealerships in east St. Louis for a lump sum of money.

I was also breaking into houses in the white people's neighborhoods. Sometimes I'd get caught and sent to juvenile detention, or to a boy's home for a couple of months. But it was worth it to me, so I didn't care. I was popular and was able to do things to take some of the load off my mother. The first few times I got locked up, she sat me down, trying to talk some sense into me, but gave up after seeing it did no good.

Other people tried steering me in the right direction, too. Some came to juvenile detention but all they told us was if we didn't stop doing what we were doing, we'd end up in prison...or dead. We acted like we were paying attention to what they were telling us, only because they brought us cookies. When they left, we laughed at them. What did they know anyway? They weren't from our 'hood, they were from the county and didn't know spit about us or the lives we lived.

I sat in Ms. Grant's classroom, #204, staring off in the distance. I could feel the weight of the semi-automatic gun I had tucked in my waist. Randy had to die. I looked over at Carlos. He wasn't a tough kid but nobody bothered him because they'd have to deal with me. And not just me but Tommy Red and KC, too. They were killers, most people in the city knew it. I liked it that way, but...

Randy had to die and I had tried to kill him. That's what Tommy Red and KC told me. "How did I get myself into this?," I thought. I didn't want to kill nobody. All I wanted was money, acceptance by my peers, not to be put down and called crazy or stupid. I put the last kid who called me stupid in Children's Hospital. By this time, I had been in lots of fights. I'd won most of them as I'd sneak up on whoever had bested me and beat them down with a pipe or brick. But I wasn't a killer and I knew it. Still...

Randy had to die. He lived the next street over and I'd seen him around the neighborhood many times, but never said anything to him. He was a few years older than me, and looked like most kids during that era - light skinned with a jerry curl. I didn't know much about him, just that he worked for KC and Tommy Red. He was bringing them in big money so I don't know why they wanted me to kill him, it didn't make sense to me. Maybe he was cooking the books, I don't know. I was scared to kill him myself as I knew I didn't have the heart to do something like that, but I knew somebody who did.

His name was Andre Morrow and he just flunked the seventh grade. His class was down the hall from mine and I started to get up from my desk and go talk to him, but thought better of it. The principal, Mr. Hammond, had already warned me that if I got in the slightest bit of trouble, I'd be kicked out of the school district. The thought of having to fight all over again to establish my reputation horrified me. Plus, those cats on the west side killed us north side dudes for sport.

I caught up with Andre after school and invited him over to my house. I made sure he knew to come to the basement door, because my mother never let company use the front door. I pulled out a bottle of Mad Dog 20/20 when he got there and we passed it back an forth is silence for a while. We drank the whole bottle and by the time we finished, we were stupid drunk. Andre loved to talk when he got drunk. I found out that evening when he started telling me about people he'd beat up or shot. By the way he was talking, I could tell he liked hurting people. I remember thinking, "This nigga crazy!"

When he finally shut up, I told him what KC and Tommy Red wanted me to do and asked him if he'd help if I paid him. He said he wasn't getting involved with them or with nothing they had going because they were snitches. That got my attention! Made me think about the times that KC and I'd get caught by the police. He never went to jail but I always ended up in juvenile detention. I caught up with KC and Tommy Red the following day and told them I wasn't going to kill Randy or anyone else for them. I said if they wanted Randy dead they had to kill him themselves. Randy was standing in his front yard a few days later when two gunmen shot him in his head and chest. That's where he died, at the feet of his grandfather.

After Randy was killed I started thinking about my own safety. If they'd kill someone they grew up with, what would they do to me? He was their right hand man, their best earner, and they blew him away like it was nothing. I could only imagine what they'd do to me. I stopped hanging around them after that. I went solo-bolo. Besides, I could make more money stealing cars and doing burglaries by myself. I let them know what was up and if they didn't like it? Oh well. I was 'Lil Cook' and had a big ass 9 mm in my waist.

We got put out of our house a month later and moved around the corner on Euclid Avenue. It was the same neighborhood so nothing really changed except my relationship with KC and Tommy Red. When I started hustling by myself they quit speaking to me. Every time one of them drove by, they'd rolled down their window and stick their arm out, making sure I got a good look at their Rolex. I also noticed detective Clide coming at me, trying to catch me with a stolen car so he could lock me up. I knew they put him on me but what could I do?

Handy Park was just around the corner from our house. It had a softball diamond, swings and merry-go-rounds but it wasn't near the size of Heman Park. Somebody told me, back when the white people lived in the area, there were more buildings in the park, even a swimming pool. I used the park as a shortcut to and from school. That's how I met Jerome Hill. He was a few years older than me, wore his hair in a jerry curl, dark skinned and weighed about 180 pounds. One day, when I was on my way to school, he was standing on his porch and we kicked up a conversation. Come to find out, we had lots of things in common, including our dislike of KC and Tommy Red. He was just getting started in the dope game but was moving up fast and would eventually become the biggest drug dealer in St. Louis. KC and Tommy Red wanted everybody who sold drugs in our neighborhood to buy it from them but Jerome was getting a better deal from somewhere and that didn't sit well with them.

Jerome and his family lived on Walton Place in two houses that sat side-by-side and I'd stop by either one before or after school and kick it with him. He was a likable guy, very book smart, and I used to wonder why someone so smart would be out there in the streets selling dope. That didn't make sense to me, and come to think of it, nothing made sense to me. Especially the night somebody tried to blow my head off.

Falicia was a beautiful girl that went to school with me and every time we passed each other in the hallway, she'd avoid me. I even tried sitting with her in the cafeteria but she moved to another table. I had sex with a couple of girls but wasn't stupid. The only reason they gave me the coochie was because I had money to buy things they wanted. Falicia was playing hard to get and that turned me on. One day I made up my mind - I was going to get her - and didn't care how much I had to pay for the coochie.

One day I was sitting in the basement when the phone rang. Falicia was calling to see if I'd skip school the next day and come over to her house. And like a damned fool, my stupid self never thought of asking how she'd gotten my phone number or why the sudden interest in me. I was so naïve. The next day I was standing at her front door with a big grin on my face. Everybody in school wanted to get into her pants and as far as I knew, nobody had. I thought about that while I was waiting for her to answer the door. I was going to school the next day and telling everyone!

When she opened the door, she was standing there with underwear on, and that did it for me. After it was over, she asked if I'd come back over later that night and like a damn fool I said, "Yeah." When I left, I went home and took a shower, then put on clean clothes. I hadn't had anything to eat since breakfast so I fixed something to eat using a microwave I stole in a burglary, then sat on the couch waiting on the sun to go down.

Falicia lived about fifteen minutes from our house, on Natural Boulevard, and that was by taking the shortcut through Handy Park. Bit if I didn't it would take half an hour to get to her house and I wasn't willing to wait that long. Walton Place ran right into the park so I had to pass Jerome's house on the way there. The lights were out so I kept walking. I was glad they weren't on, to tell the truth, because I didn't want to stop there anyway.

The park was so dark at night that if you put your hand in front of your face, you won't be able to see it. I walked through it almost every night, but this night was different. I felt in my gut that something was terribly wrong. I grew so nervous that my legs gave out. While I was falling, I saw a silver blur followed by gunshots. Whoever it was shooting at me must have misjudged the distance or maybe my legs giving out saved my life. I didn't stick around trying to figure it out, I was up and running towards Jerome's house. Whoever was after me could run faster than I could because I heard footsteps gaining on me. Halfway to Jerome's house I saw him run outside and start firing at whoever was chasing me. I ducked down behind a car, then looked back to see who was shooting at me and I recognized the face. It was detective Clide!

CHAPTER 7: MISCHIEF MAKER

"Happy is the man that feareth always; but
he that hardeneth his heart shall fall
into mischief." - Prov. 28:14

I could hear sirens blaring, getting louder with each step I took. I was
running through the tree-lined streets of Clayton, Missouri. The sirens
were coming from police cars, not ambulances. The police in those cars
were looking to capture a sixteen-year-old fugitive who had, just minutes
before, escaped from the St. Louis County Detention Center. I was that
fugitive and was running with only a pair of underwear, socks and a t-
shirt on. I could feel the wind picking up and it was raining. I was getting
cold. A few minutes before, I'd been locked up in an isolated unit by
myself. None of the kids at the detention center were allowed to speak to
me. I was too dangerous.

I took my glasses off and wiped the rain from them, all while
desperately looking for somewhere to hide. I was in pretty good shape
but after running flat-out for fifteen minutes, I was exhausted. Clayton
was one of the richest counties in Missouri, and that meant lots of white
people, no black people and no alleys. I was winded and the pain in my
side was becoming unbearable. I saw street lights up ahead and that gave
me some hope, and a little more wind. I could see a gas station a block
away, on the corner streets that separated Clayton from University City. I
started running faster and soon passed the gas station and ran into an
alley.

Until that night, I'd never been inside a dumpster. I'd hurdled bricks and rocks at them but never even look inside. This night changed that because the first thing I saw when I turned into the alley was a big beige dumpster. I lifted the lid, climbed in, and was greeted by the smell of rotten food. I closed the lid and sat down, hoping there were no rats in there. I loved mice but I couldn't stand rats. I didn't hear anything moving around, just the sound of my heartbeat. I could still hear sirens but could tell they were getting fainter with each passing second. I reached own, rubbing my sore feet. They were hurting so bad and I felt pain throughout my lower body. My suspicion was confirmed when I brought my hand to my nose - my feet were bleeding. I pulled the bloody socks off and started picking the rocks out of my feet, one by one.

After detective Clide shot at me that night, I tried keeping a low profile. Falicia had set me up and I didn't wanted to go to school the following day and beat her down. A friend told me KC and Tommy Red paid detective Clide to kill me because I stopped hustling with them and they were upset because they weren't bringing in as much money as before. I kept stealing cars and breaking into houses for the next year and a half, and trying to knock KC and Tommy Red's head off every chance I got.

The police busted me in 1986 and sent me to a boy's home in mid-downtown St. Louis called Hogan Street. My mother's boyfriend at the time, Jesse Aldridge, was cool with Mr. Bailey, the youth leader of the group home I was in. Mr. Bailey told me I was a smart kid with a bright future ahead of me and that I should enroll in the St. Louis City Job Corps when I was released. There was a black woman working there that I had a serious crush on. Her name was Vanita Hill. She was in her late twenties, had light brown skin, was smart and had the most amazing figure. I was in love with her and made sure she knew it. I told her I wanted to come see her when I was released and she gave ne her phone number and address.

I was released from Hogan Street in the spring of 1987, and enrolled in the Job Corps. It sat in the middle of the city where most of the drugs were bought and sold. That was a problem for me because by this time I was smoking week and PCP. I can't remember if I even went to class the whole time I was there because I was high all the time. I do remember making a few friends while I was there, Danielle Patterson, Lisa Ewing and Pedro Williams. Pedro was a short, skinny, brown skinned black kid with a monstrous sense of humor. We were together almost everyday, riding around in stolen cars and getting high. That's what we were doing one day in Welston, Missouri - getting high as a kite - when the police got behind us. I made a quick left turn and pulled over. Then we hopped out of the car and ran. Pedro got away but I wasn't so lucky. I got caught and sent to the St. Louis County Juvenile Detention Center on Brentwood Boulevard.

The county juvenile was different from the city's in many ways. The first thing that I noticed was it was much cleaner, bigger an had more white people working there. The food was better, library bigger and the boys could sometimes mingle with the girls. The unit I was in had ten kids in it, most were white. There was only one black kid besides myself. There was a day room that had plastic chairs in it where we could play cards but I never played. I had one thing on my mind and one thing only...escaping.

I kept my eyes and ears open, looking for a way out of there. I played sick sometimes because the unit leader let me go to the medical unit alone. That gave me an opportunity to look around at most of the building. One day I was talking to this kid who told me about the medial center across the street from the detention center. He said if we needed to get our teeth cleaned, we'd get escorted there by a deputy juvenile deputy (DJO). I was surprised when he said that they didn't cuff us when we went. That's all I needed to hear, I was getting out of there. The next day I filled out a request to have my teeth cleaned and a couple days later was escorted by the DJO to the medical center. I started to cut out from him when we first walked out the door but I knew if I did, I'd most likely get caught. So I waited for just the right moment. It came when we were in the waiting room and the DJO said he needed to use the bathroom and that he'd be right back. When he left, I started looking around the room and saw a window open. I climbed through it and took off down Brentwood Boulevard.

I knew I couldn't go home because that's the first place the police would look. And I couldn't stay on the streets, either. Not in Clayton, Missouri. White people were staring and pointing their fingers at me the whole time I was running and I knew it was just a matter of time before one of them called the police. The problem, for me at least, was Clayton, Missouri had no alleys. I could get around there being a black face on the streets, that was easy, but it's much easier getting away from the police in alleys because they wouldn't come into them alone. They'd wait for backup and by the time they got there, I'd be long gone. I ran for a while, looking behind me and when I turned a corner, a police officer was waiting for me with his gun pointed at my head.

I was cuffed and put in a police van, then took back to the detention center. When I got there they put me in the hole where I stayed a couple of weeks, and was then let out and put back in the same unit I was in before. A week later I told the unit leader I wasn't feeling well and needed to see a nurse. When he opened the unit's door I walked towards the medical unit but when I heard the door close behind me, I ran down the steps to the gym. I grabbed a baseball bat when I got there and busted a window out. I walked outside and found myself staring at a huge concrete wall. I didn't know what to do at that point so I stood there for a minute, trying to figure out how to get over it. I went back inside the gym and looked around. There was a wooden door to the right that opened to a room where the athletic equipment was kept. I ran to it and twisted the knob but it was locked. I turned to go back outside when something caught my eye. The volleyball net, wrapped around a steel pole. I ran and grabbed it, took it outside and laid it up against the wall. I started climbing up and a few seconds later, I was over the wall.

But I got caught and that's the reason I found myself hiding in a dumpster, bare feet, wet and cold wearing just my underwear, socks and a t-shirt. I had escaped again. The sirens faded so I lifted the lid and climbed out into the alley. I didn't know what neighborhood I was in but I knew it was in University City. Big Bend Boulevard was just a couple blocks away so I started walking in that direction. I didn't have far to walk because George lived just a half a mile away, but man my feet were killing me!

I stood at the front door looking around. George's station wagon wasn't in the driveway but I knocked on the door anyway. Nobody answered so I sat on the porch, figuring on waiting until he got home because I had nowhere to go. Even if I did, my feet were hurting so bad I couldn't take another step. Then I heard the sirens growing nearer so I put my head down and started crying. Diane would be so disappointed in me.

CHAPTER 8: JAILBOUND

"For they considered not the miracle
of the loaves: for their heart was hardened." - Mark 6:52

After escaping from the county juvenile, they had had enough of me. The DJO told me if it had been just one escape, I would've received a few months in a boy's home. But since I'd repeatedly done it, they had no choice but to certify me to stand trial as an adult. I was on my way to prison. I was already locked up for burglaries and tampering with motor vehicles and once I get sent to the county jail, and fingerprinted, all kinds of crimes I'd committed would pop up.

My original court date was months away but was moved up because I was considered an escape risk. I sat in the holding tank, waiting on them to come and get me for my hearing. There was a guard outside the door to make sure I didn't run off again. I knew I was in big trouble when the door opened and three officers walked in. Not because it was three of them but because they all carried guns. They were real police and not the average, everyday detention officers. I was cuffed and escorted to the courtroom. The judge said a few words and that was it. I don't think the proceeding was even legal. But legal or not, it worked because as soon as it was over I was taken straight to the St. Louis County Jail.

I didn't stay there long because I was only sixteen-years-old and they didn't want anything to happen to me. I wasn't actually an adult, they'd just certified me as one. I was one of the first groups of juveniles in Missouri to get certified to stand trial as an adult. It was easy to convince us to accept whatever plea bargain the prosecutor offered because we didn't know a thing about the law. For me, it was plead guilty to fourteen felonies, get sentenced to 11 seven year sentences and three year sentences. The three year sentences and seven year sentences would be served consecutive of each other. I don't know why they make these types of things so complicated. I get confused trying to explain it all! The bottom line was, I got a total of 10 years to be served in the Missouri Department of Corrections.

After getting my time, I was transferred to a jail in Chesterfield, Missouri (I forget the name but we called it 'Gumbo'). I was put in a cell by myself because even though I was certified an adult, I was still a child. The cells looked like the ones in juvenile, steel everything including the bed. My cell was in a segregated part of the jail, on what became known as the juvenile floor. This area housed juveniles who had been certified by the city or county courts. We had to stay there until our seventeenth birthday, then we'd be sent to a regular cell block. I was turning seventeen a couple of months after I got there, and when I did, I was put in a regular unit. I stayed there for three short months before being transferred to Fulton Reception and Diagnostic Center (FRDCC) on January 3, 1988. I was chained together with several other inmates and put into a white van for the two hour drive to FRDCC. They were older than me and I didn't know any of them. I didn't say a word the whole trip but I listened to them talk about different prisons they'd been in. I could tell just by the way they were talking that I was in for a hell of a ride.

When the van pulled in front of the prison, I was shocked beyond words. The whole prison looked as if it was made out of razor wire. Whatever plans I had of escaping was dead on arrival. The van stopped in an enclosure surrounded by razor wire. We filed out of the van and told to keep our mouths shut and follow an officer into the building. Inside, we were stripped naked, sprayed with chemicals and given a ten minute shower. We couldn't keep our personal clothing so were given the option of sending it home or donating it to charity. I donated everything because I didn't have any money for postage.

They made us stand in the hallway naked while we were fingerprinted and processed in. Afterwards, we were assigned to housing units to stay until they figured out what prison we'd be sent to. Man, I tell you, that place was crazy! Half of the inmates walked around all day talking to themselves. People were getting stabbed and raped, all on just a few acres of land. That's the part that bothered me the most. If somebody got after me, there was nowhere to run unless you count running in circles.

Whatever you did on the streets was just that - on the streets. 'Lil Cook didn't mean nothing in that place. In there, you had to either fight, succumb to being raped or check in. My cellmate was a black guy in his thirties who first came to prison in his twenties. He seemed pretty cool but I still kept one eye open just in case he tried something sneaky. He called himself a 'Moorish American Muslim' and said he was a follower of Noble Drew Ali, the black man who founded the Moorish Science Temple of America

(MSTA). Noble Drew Ali (formally Timothy Drew) was born in Newark, New Jersey in the late 1800s and in early 1900 claimed to be the last prophet, and that Allah sent him to save the 'Asiatic's of North America' (black people) from their 'European Oppressors' (white people). He literally claimed he was Jesus incarnate. The 'Moors', as they were called, claimed that whites had stolen the Moorish flag from Africa and Noble Drew Ali went to the White House, found it in the basement, then took it and place it in their Temple. Throughout my time in prison, I asked many Moors, including my cellmate, the whereabouts of the flag but they told me it was a secret.

The Moors wore fez hats, combat boots and greeted another saying, "Peace Moor." Noble Drew Ali wrote a sixty page Koran he claimed Allah inspired him to write. He printed it out and gave each member a 'Nationality Card' with their name on it. He said the reason white people treated blacks the way they did was because we (blacks) didn't know and or proclaim our nationality and 'divine creed.' The Moors said that if we proclaimed our nationality and divine creed, the white man would recognize us as real citizens and wouldn't treat us bad anymore.

I spent two months at FRDCC without any problems with other inmates. While I was there, I took a lengthy diagnostic test to determine what prison I'd be sent to. There were math, science, reading and psychological tests. There was no passing grade, which I didn't understand, but took it anyway. I did terrible in every area except reading. The lady who gave the test said my reading was that of a first year college student's. That made me feel kind of good but also bad, because I knew the only reason I'd scored high was because of Diane.

They came for me in the wee hours and told me to pack my belongings because I was getting transferred to Boonville Correctional Center (BCC) in Boonville, Missouri. Me and forty-four inmates were loaded into a big gray prison bus called 'The Gray Goose' for the two-hour trip. I sat in the back and watched the car tailing the bus for a while, then gazed out the window. There were farms everywhere and I sat wishing I was living in one of them, wishing I was anywhere but on that bus.

I knew I was in trouble as soon as we pulled into the gates because there were gangs of inmates standing around, checking us out. I'd already heard cat-calls and we hadn't even stepped off the bus yet. The cat-calls didn't bother me. What bothered me was there were several in the crowd who I'd jumped on our shot at on the streets in St. Louis. And they weren't yelling or talking about no tail, either. They were saying they were going to kill me. Some of them were guys who worked for KC or Tommy Red and I could tell by the bulges in their waists that they had shanks on them. If the officers hadn't been standing there with guns and rifles, I'd be dead for sure.

I learned from another inmate that orientation lasted for two weeks.

That's all the time I had to figure something out. I didn't have a problem fighting anybody. In fact back then, I welcomed it. But there were too many of those cats and they had knives. I was in the TV room when I overheard an inmate mention the name of an old friend, Sean Lewis. He didn't call him that, he used his nickname "Nookie." He lived on Northland Avenue and was the one who told me KC and Tommy Red asked detective Clide to kill me that night in Handy Park.

I sent Nookie a kite through a food service worker, telling him what was going on and that I needed a knife as soon I got to the general population (GP). He sent a kite the next day saying, "Everything's taken care of, don't worry." Most of the inmates were young black men in their 20s and 30s, with me being the only teenager. One of the first things I learned about [prison was that it's totally different from the streets. Nookie was a killer and even KC and Tommy Red's crew wouldn't mess with him. If you got into it in prison you either beat them down, stabbed them or killed them. There was no running, unless you went to protective custody (PC) and then your reputation would be ruined.

The first couple of months I was there, I hung out with Nookie and a few guys I knew from the streets. I didn't get any visits but called and wrote home regularly. My old girlfriend Monica sent me a letter saying she'd given birth to a baby girl and that I was the father. She named her Melinda (MeMe). She is light skinned so I didn't think I was the father. I sent a letter and a DNA sample to the Missouri Highway Patrol requesting they examine me to see if I was the father and come to find out, I was.

Nookie was supposed to be released in the spring of 1989 but the parole board took his date away because the night before he was to leave, he jumped on a white guy and messed him up really bad. He was put in the hole for a few months, then transferred to Missouri State Penitentiary (MSP). When word of that got to KC and Tommy Red's crew, they came after me. I never thought that would happen because of Nookie but when he was gone, I was alone. I stabbed inmates, inmates stabbed me. I beat inmates, inmates beat me. Finally the administration got tired of me and sent me to another prison in Missouri. I was only there a couple of months and got a visit from my mother, my sister Tammy and my daughter MeMe. This was the first and only time I ever held my daughter in my arms. She was close to her first birthday and when I held her, and she spit gook on me.

CHAPTER 9: BLOODY 40 ACRES

"Then he said unto me, The iniquity of the house of
Israel and Judah is exceeding great, and the land is
full of blood, and the city full of perverseness: for
they say, the Lord hath forsaken the earth, and the
Lord seeth not." - Ezek. 9:9

I didn't stay at the prison in Moberly for long, and was transferred to
MSP. They called it "Bloody 40 Acres," and it was indeed bloody. I was
there for a year and a half and during that time, watched many inmates kill
each other. I couldn't believe what I saw. I'd heard about MSP and all the
horror stories but hearing and seeing it with my own two eyes was
something else. It's terrible seeing a woman getting raped but can you
imagine watching a man?

When I walked into the receiving area, there was a brass sign hanging
on the wall that read: "Leave All Your Hopes and Dreams Behind." I
stopped and stared at it for a minute, wondering what it meant. After being
processed, I was escorted to Super Max, the most isolated administrative
segregation unit in the Department of Corrections. The cell I was put in
was made of concrete with the exception of the steel toilet and sink. The
bed was a two feet high slab of concrete running the length of the back
wall. The toilet was backed up and the walls seeped when it rained. There
wasn't a mattress in the cell so when the officer came by I asked if he'd get
me one. He told me I had to earn one by being a good little boy. I gave him
the finger and he gave me his billy club.

I sat in Super Max everyday, staring out the back window. And
everyday I saw the same thing. A guard with a machine gun standing on top
a thirty feet concrete wall. Super Max was quiet for the most part but there

were times I heard an inmate scream in the agony of losing his sanity. I was released after three months and sent to GP. The officer who escorted me told me I was going to housing unit number two. I was glad to hear that because I'd heard that that unit was single-man cells.

MSP was located in the heart of Jefferson City, Missouri, and was the oldest prison in the state. The outlaw Jesse James and James Earl Ray were a couple of its most infamous inmates. It had a population of 2,500, including death row inmates. Most were serving life without parole or its equivalent. There were people who'd never see the free world again. And then there was me.

I laid in my bunk with wet toilet tissue stuffed in both ears. I tried turning the radio up, putting a pillow over my head, but nothing drowned out the screams. I wanted to go to the yard and library to find out what house Nookie was in but by the time I finished unpacking, the yard was closed. So I laid down to get some sleep. After the 10 p.m. custody count, an officer came by each inmate's cell and asked if he wanted to visit another inmate. I told him I was cool. Who was I going to visit? I heard several cell doors open and close, then the noises and screams came. That was the first time in my life I cursed to God.

I didn't get any sleep that night. If it wasn't for the sounds, it was the smell. I washed my face and brushed my teeth, then headed to the dining hall, looking for Nookie. I found him there and we hugged, then I told him what went down the night before and that I needed a shank. Our conversation was interrupted by a loud scream. We turned to see what was going on and saw an inmate getting stabbed by several people. He was trying to run but every direction he went, someone was there waiting. They kept stabbing him until he fell to the ground. I looked at the officer who was witnessing the whole thing, he was acting as if nothing was going on.

At the time, I was the youngest inmate to be transferred to MSP. I knew that and so did everyone else. I saw inmates we called 'booty bandits,' watching me all the time but they never bothered me. Maybe because they knew I carried a shank everywhere I went or that they didn't want to have to deal with Nookie. Whatever the reason, I was glad they left me alone.

Almost every day I sat in the yard and watched a group of black inmates called 'Black Muslims.' They were the ones who separated from the Nation of Islam after the death of its leader, Elijah Muhammad, in the 1970s. They were supposed to follow the orthodox version of Islam and while that may have been the case in the free world, it wasn't in prison. The Black Muslims hated white people and refused to allow any of them to join their organization.

Then there was the Nation of Islam who were under the leadership of Louis Farrakhan. Minister Farrakhan was a student of the slain civil rights leader Malcolm X but then Malcolm left the Nation of Islam and joined the orthodox Muslim community. Minister Farrakhan labeled him a traitor and not only cut ties with Malcolm, but said he was "worthy of death." Some historians believe Minister Farrakhan and the Nation of Islam assassinated Malcolm and other say it was the United States Government. I should mention that both Minister Farrakhan and the government deny any involvement in the killing.

The Nation of Islam, the Black Muslims, Moorish Science Temple, Black Panther Party and other smaller, lesser-know organizations united and formed The Black Muslim Movement. They realized there were strength in numbers and became a force to be reckoned with inside the prisons and I found that attractive. I saw their power, the fear in the white inmates and guards whenever they were around. They could do anything they wanted - beat you down, stab you, kill you - and nothing would be said or done about it.

They gathered in the yard and chanted "Black Power" and other things that were supposed to encourage and uplift black people. Hundreds of black inmates would sit on the yard, listening to speaker after speaker. I never saw so many black people together where something didn't get hurt or killed. That was a real shocker but what really got to me was their preaching of and the embracing and love for their black skin. They talked on and on how beautiful it was to be black and that white people were the devil.

I asked one of them how could white be devils when I probably would've starved to death if it wasn't for Pete the fireman. I shared with them how Pete fed me and played with me whenever I wanted. The guy I talked to said, "White people are like snakes, some poisonous, some not. And since black people don't know nothing about snakes, it's best to treat them all like they're poisonous."

It seemed that The Black Muslims had the answers to ever question I had in life. I asked how I could join and was told I'd have to "get down on one of them white devils." I had a few fights with white kids in juvenile but it wasn't because of the color of their skin. What he was asking me to do didn't sit well with me but I wanted to be somebody. I wanted to matter.

I started beating white Christians because they said Christianity was the "white devil" religion, and we had to stop it from spreading. They told me I had to stab one of them, so I did. And the next thing I knew I was beating, stabbing and robbing then regularly. I moved up the ranks pretty fast and before long, became their leader. I remember one Christian I'd robbed and confined to his cell. I refused him a shower, wouldn't allow him to brush his teeth, comb his hair or even eat. He lost dozens of pounds and the last time I saw him he was digging through the trash can looking for something to eat. I walked by and laughed, not realizing at the time, twenty years later, I'd be a crack addict digging in a trash can looking for something to eat myself.

I loved reading and even after Diane passed away, I kept at it, reading everything I could get my hands on. Sometimes when I broke into houses in wealthy neighborhoods, I'd steal books from their libraries. Prior to joining The Black Muslim Movement, I'd never read a book by a black author. When its members gave me books to read, they were all the same - black this and black that. I quickly grew tired of them and made a point of going to the prison library to check out books on different topics. I read everything - westerns, science, mathematics - whatever books I could. I even thought about reading on of the Bibles on the shelf but didn't want to read nothing about the white man's God.

The library was open seven days a week and I went there every chance I got. That's how I ran into Ms. Grieger. She was an old white woman in her seventies who retired from teaching school to come into the prison to help inmates get their GED. She stood under five feet, had white hair and a wrinkled face. Most of the time when I went to the library, I'd see her standing in the hallway staring at me.

One day I was leaving the library and she stopped me and introduced herself, asking if I wanted to attend her class. I told her, "No, I don't want or need no white man's education," then walked away. "God bless you" I heard behind me. I snapped, calling her and God every disgusting thing I could think of. I laid in my bunk that night thinking about Diane. I always tried not to do that because it made me cry. Whenever I had thoughts of her, I read books to get my mind off her, but that night it didn't work. Even though Ms. Grieger was white and Diane was black, the look on Ms. Grieger's face earlier that day was the same look I'd seen on Diane's - a look that said, "I care."

The next day I didn't go to the library, I went to Ms. Grieger's classroom. When I walked in, she was sitting at her desk doing paperwork. "Can I speak to you for a minute?" I asked. She looked up, smiled, and invited me in. I sat in a chair next to her desk and apologized for cursing her out, then asked if she'd accept my apology. She said, "Of course," then the two of us sat in silence for a while. I didn't know what to say because I'd never really had a conversation with a white woman.

"I've noticed you like reading," she said. I responded, "Yeah." She started asking questions like how far I got in school? Did I have a favorite teacher? Who were my friends? I can't remember how I answered about my friends but I did tell her I made it to the ninth grade. "God has a plan for you, do you know that Anthony?" she said. I'd been trained to instinctively respond a certain way when asked that kind of thing but I couldn't say a word that day. I wanted to curse her out so bad but she reached over, grabbed my hand, and squeezed. it.

I sat in the visiting room, waiting on Monica. I met her through

Danielle when we were in Job Corps and it had been years since I'd seen her. She was short, dark skinned and wore her hair in a perm.

She walked into the visiting room and sat down in a chair next to me. We talked for a while, then she brought up the letter I got from her a couple weeks before. I had been sitting in my cell studying for the GED when an officer handed me a letter. It was from Monica. I sat there for a minute, wondering if it was like the others I'd received from her before, the ones that left me feeling sick.

I sat there looking at her. She was a woman I loved once but that day, I didn't know how I felt about her. She wanted me to have her boyfriend killed. That was what the letter was about. I could've had it done but didn't want to. I'd told her in letters and on the phone that I was studying for the GED so I could get a good job and take care of MeMe when I got out of prison. I couldn't believe she asked me to do something like that.

Nookie was dead. He got out a couple months before and was gunned down by Tommy Red and KC. Pedro Williams, Andre Morrow and my brother Demetrice were all in prison. It seemed as if everybody I was cool with was either locked up or dead. I told Monica if she was having so much trouble out of her boyfriend, she should put him out of the house, but I wasn't getting involved. She got upset and started cursing me out. Told me I'd better get it done or she'd make sure I never saw my daughter again. I got up and walked out the door.

CHAPTER 10: THE CHASE

"For they being ignorant of God's righteousness,
and going about to establish their own
righteousness, have not submitted
themselves unto the righteousness of God." - Rom. 10:3

"Keep your head up brother minister!" I heard on my way out the door. I'd been in prison for six years and eight months and was on my way home. I was transferred from MSP because my custody level had dropped from maximum to minimum security. I spent my last eighteen months at Farmington Correctional Center (FCC) and hated it because I'd grown to like Ms. Grieger, even though I had to hear her everyday trying to get me to turn my life over to some white man named Jesus.

An officer drove me to a bus station in town where I purchased a one-way ticket to St. Louis. The bus station looked like the liquor stores that sat on every corner in my neighborhood. The floor and counter were wooden, there were dozens of bags of potato chips hanging behind the counter. People were walking around everywhere I looked. I found that strange because it had been so long since I'd seen something like that. I felt like a new born baby, trying to figure out what I was seeing.

The bus pulled up and I got on, then took a seat in the back. I could feel the vibration on the big engine when it started moving. It felt weird sitting there with people who weren't chained together. The scent of perfume, a baby crying...it was like I fell asleep and woke up on another planet. I looked out the window at cars rolling up and down the highway, trying to figure out the cars' makes and models. I recognized some that I saw on television but to see them in real life was something else. I settled in my seat and thought about my brother Tim who'd be waiting on me at the bus station in St. Louis. He was just fifteen-years-old when I went to prison but now he was twenty-one with his own apartment and car. The trip would take ninety minutes, giving me lots of time to think.

My older brother Demetrice was in prison and younger sister Tammy had become a stripper working in the strip clubs in East St. Louis. My mother had moved from the apartment on Euclid Avenue to an apartment in north St. Louis on Pauline Place. She also had a new boyfriend named James and I thought that was funny because it seemed as if every man she had was named James. Just thinking about her brought tears to my eyes, I'd missed her so much. I only got one visit from her the whole time I was locked up. She wanted to come more often but every prison I was in was too far for her to drive.

I saw Tim smiling while looking at me through the window, when the bus pulled into the parking lot. He looked so grown up with a mustache and beard. I got off, we hugged, then got in his car. I asked how our mother was doing and he didn't say anything. I asked a second time. "Alright, I guess." he said. I looked out the window, surprised at how the city had changed. There were new businesses, new streets and some of the streets I used to hang out on were completely gone. Even the people looked different somehow. I also noticed there were more run-down neighborhoods and vacant lots than there were when I left. It looked like a war zone.

We turned on Pauline Place and I could tell what kind of neighborhood it was just by watching people who were standing around on the sidewalks and in gangways. There were apartments on both sides of the street and trash scattered everywhere. Tim parked in front of the apartment, we got out and walked up the stairs to the front door.

"Hey baby!" my mother said, jumping into my arms. We hugged, cried, then sat on the couch and talked for a while. She told me what I already knew - Tammy working at a strip club and Demetrice being in prison for burglary. She said she had to use the bathroom, then got up and headed down the hall. Tim said he had a run to make and he would be back soon. I heard the door closed then looked around the room. It didn't look nice as it did on the pictures I had received in prison. The furniture was old and had holes in them. Tim had bought me some new clothes so while my mother was in the bathroom, I took off the prison dress-outs and put my new clothes on.

I figured my mother went to the kitchen to cook something to eat because she'd been gone for nearly an hour. I had to use the bathroom myself plus I wanted to look around the apartment. I walked down the hallway and noticed the bathroom door open. When I stepped in, I found her on the floor with a crack pipe and Bic lighter laying beside her. I picked her up, took her to the living room, and sat her on the couch. She was breathing okay but her eyes were wide open, staring at nothing.

Time came through the door and I told him how I found her and what had happened. "She cool Tony my man, she just high." he said. I looked down at her and back at him, not believing what I heard. I knew she smoked a little weed bit it didn't affect people like that. When she came down from her high, she told me she smoked crack "here and there" but wasn't hooked on it. I heard about crack and the affect it had on people when I was in prison, and I knew it wasn't something you quit whenever you felt like it.

I wanted to take my mind off of the subject so I shared with them my plans for the future, my plans of getting a job and taking care of MeMe. My mother said she hadn't seen MeMe in a while but knew she lived on St. Louis Avenue and 69th Street with Monica's mother. We talked for a while longer, then I told them I was going to see MeMe. I gave them a hug and left. I walked towards the bus stop on Union Boulevard. I couldn't get the image of my mother laying on the bathroom floor out of my head. When I was in prison, I saw movies with women on their hands and knees having sex with a dog, just for a hit of crack. I felt tears rolling down my face as I looked back to see if the bus was coming. It wasn't. When it finally came, I got on and went to the back and sat down, not wanting to be bothered by other passengers.

I had to catch three different buses to get to the neighborhood where she lived, then I had to walk a few more blocks. It was dark by the time I got there. I stood on the corner of 69th Street and watched a few guys standing around a car looking like they were making a drug transaction. It was cold and the snow began to fall but I waited until they finished doing their thing before I walked down the street. when they left, I went to the house and knocked on the door.

An older black woman answered and I asked what I wanted to ask. I told her who I was and that I was there to see MeMe. She let me into the living room and said I had to wait there while she went to get her. I stood there looking around. There was a couch and a lounge chair. The floor was wood with cracks in it from one side of the room to the other. I could see the dining area, an old table missing its leg on it. The old woman who let me in was MeMe's grandmother and she said she didn't think my daughter would be happy to see me. I kept my mouth shut because I didn't know why she said that or how I should respond to it. MeMe walked into the room and my heartbeat went sky high. At just six-years-old I could tell she would grow up to be a beautiful woman. She was short, a little on the chubby side, light skinned and wore her hair in braids. "Who are you?" she asked me. I said, "I'm your father, Anthony. I just got out of prison earlier today and..." before I could finish, she started screaming, then turned and ran from the room calling for her grandmother.

My first hit of crack blew my mind. I'd smoked weed and PCP but they didn't make me feel the way crack did. When I inhaled the smoke, it buckled my knees and took my breath away. Despite this, I wanted more, couldn't get enough no matter how much I had. It made me feel so good, took the pain away and I didn't worry about anything. Why had MeMe screamed and ran away from me? Who cared? All I cared about was getting high again.

I looked at Lisa, who was on her hands and knees searching the floor to see if we'd dropped any crumbs of crack. When I left my daughter, I walked around the city trying to figure out what to do next. I didn't want to go back to my mother's place because I was too afraid of what I might see. I found myself walking in the neighborhood where an old friend used to live, so I stopped by. Her name was Lisa and now here we were in a vacant house smoking crack and running out of money.

She wanted to take the few dollars we had left and buy more crack, but I suggested we rent a car and go burglarize a house, that way we'd have enough money to keep us high. We walked around her neighborhood until we ran into a guy she knew who said he'd rent us his car for $20. We gave him the money, got the keys, and hopped in with me at the wheel. It was an old 1986 hard-body Ford that was missing its radio. I started the engine, then we drove off and the next thing I knew Lisa yelled, "Watch that car Anthony! They're gaining on us!" She was right, they *were* gaining on us because I could hear the sirens getting closer and closer. We were driving down Kings Highway, coming from the south side where we'd just broke into a house. It was the second one we hit in less than twenty-four hours. My heart was pounding like it would bust out of my chest. I looked over at her, slowed, made a right turn and a short left, then floored it going over a hundred miles an hour on Euclid Avenue.

Lisa was the first person I hooked up with when I got out of prison and that wasn't saying much since I'd only been out for less than two days and had already found myself in a high speed chase. She was a very beautiful woman on the outside but just as ugly as me on the inside. I met her through Danielle when we were at Job Corps and we became good friends. I used to go over to her house and drink and smoke weed all day. Her mother didn't mind just as long as she got her cut.

"Watch that car!" she yelled. But it was too late. We collided with a car that was pulling away from the curb. My head slammed into the windshield, shattering my glasses. We hit another car and the impact sent me flying through the windshield and landing on a parking lot forty feet away. I lay on the ground for a minute, not believing I was alive. I looked where the car we were driving in was and it had rolled to a stop. Lisa was being drug out by a police officer. I had just seconds before they'd realize the driver was missing. I was on a parking lot so there were cars I could use for cover, one being just a few feet away so I started crawling towards it.

"Nigga, don't move!" the officer yelled from the edge of the parking lot. I saw the gun in his hands but thought I could still get away by using the cars as cover. I got up running but felt pain in my ankle, and then I heard the sound of gunshots. I fell to the ground, unable to move my head. "I'm ready to die." I thought.

I didn't die that night but was taken to the city jail and booked for tampering and traffic tickets. I also found out that the car we were in was stolen during a home invasion in St. Louis county. We told the police how we got it, that we rented it from a guy in Lisa's neighborhood, but they weren't buying our story. During the crash, Lisa had been busted up really bad, so they took her to Barnes Hospital where she escaped from. I was placed in a four-man cell to wait for St. Louis county police to come pick me up.

The cell was huge, big enough to hold at least ten people, but there were just three of us in it. The other two were a pair of St. Louis' most notorious drug dealers, Jerry Lew-Bey and Paul Leisure. One black, one Italian. Jerry Lewis-Bey was the Grand Sheik of the Moorish Science Temple of America (MSTofA) and Paul Leisure was the godfather of the Leisure family. Jerry Lewis-Bey had already been sentenced to life without parole in the federal courts for multiple counts of narcotic's trafficking and murder and so had Paul Leisure. They had been transferred to the city to stand trial at the state level. I didn't want to be in there with them and moved down the hall as soon as I could.

A couple hours later I was picked up by the St. Louis county police and transferred to Jennings police department for interrogation. When I got there I was led to a small room that had three steel chairs and a table in it. One of the detectives sat a piece of paper on the table and told me to sign it. I picked it up and read it. It was a confession. I sat it back down and told him I wasn't confessing to something I didn't do. I gave them the same story I'd given the city police and was told I had better sign the confession "if you know what's good for you." I refused and they beat me with their billy clubs.

The city had taken the traffic charges 'under advisory,' meaning they would wait to see what my parole officer wanted to do with me. Since I didn't confess to the county police and couldn't be identified in the home invasion, they were forced to release me. I left the police department and started the long walk back to the city. My parole officer would see my arrest in her computer the next morning and send me back to prison on the next thing smoking.

CHAPTER 11: OAKLAND, CALIFORNIA

"Reproach hath broken my heart; and I am full
of heaviness: and I looked for someone to take
pity, but there was no one; and for comforters,
but I found none." - Ps. 69:20

I walked so long it felt like I'd pass out. My ankles were throbbing and my feet were sore. I made it back to the north side but still had a ways to go before I reached someone's house that I knew. I was tired and hungry, having went two days without food and I couldn't remember the last time I had a drink of water. I was close to where Vanita Hill lived, or used to live, at 2020 E. Warne Avenue, so that's where I headed.

"Are you sure you're okay, Anthony?" We were sitting in her apartment at the kitchen table. Vanita was a good hearted woman, and I had a major crush on her when I was in Hogan Street Boy's Home. "Yeah, I'm alright," I said. I could tell by the look in her eyes that she knew I was lying. She was a very attractive woman. A little over five feet tall, short hair and creamy brown skin. She was the first woman I ever kissed. When we were in the library alone, I snuck one in on her. I couldn't help it! She was so beautiful!

"Let me fix you something to eat." she said, rising from the table. I glanced around. The kitchen looked the same way it did when I visited her in the mid-eighties. So did she, as if she hadn't aged a single day.

She went to the stove and started cooking a hamburger and French fries. My stomach started rumbling. "I've been praying for you over the years. Did you know that, Anthony?" she said while looking over

51

shoulder at me.

"You'll be alright baby, the Lord's going to take good care of you. Now eat your food while I see if I can find some clean clothes for you to put on," she said, setting the large plate of food on the table in front of me. I was finished eating by the time she returned. She handed me an arm full of clothes and said she'd ran a bath for me, and after I finished cleaning myself, she'd braid my hair.

It was cold and dark outside when I left her house. I had a couple hundred dollars in my pocket that she gave me to buy a bus ticket out of town. She asked what city I was headed to but I told her I didn't know, I just wanted out of St. Louis. It's true what they say – we are creatures of habit. My mind wasn't working off what it knew of the present but of the past. It couldn't have been any other way because I hadn't been in St. Louis in years. I didn't know the city or its people. A past that didn't exist.

I was never good at shooting craps. I played during my teens, just twice, and both times I lost all my money. That was it for me, my craps career over. Demetrice and a few of his friends would get together on weekends and shoot until one of them was left holding all the money, and most of the time it was a skinny, baldheaded kid named Pops. Pops and Demetrice had become friends when they were in the Job Corps in Clearfield, Utah. They didn't graduate because they got kicked out for smuggling alcohol on campus. They were bused back to St. Louis on the first thing, smoking. Pops lived not far from Vanita's house, on Hook Avenue, and that's where I was going.

I didn't want to be a target of gangbangers so I walked through the alleys. I had to be careful because they were killing everybody. I should've reached his house in a half of an hour but it took tice as long because my ankles were still sore. The wind had picked up and I was starting to get cold. I ran across Highway 70, walked up a hill, and down two more alleys to get to his street. When I came out of the last alley onto Hook Avenue, the street was quiet. Too quiet for me. There's something about a quiet street in the ghetto. The people living in one will tell you they'd rather hear loud radios or even gunshots, than be tortured by silence. I walked to the end of the street and stopped, looking to see if there were any police around. I didn't see any so I ran up to Pop's house and rang the doorbell. Despite the cold, I was sweating. "Who is it?" a woman said through the door. I yelled, "Anthony!" waiting for the door to open. I stood there nervously looking up and down the street. I prayed, "Allah, please let this woman open this door!" I gave her my name and couldn't figure out why it was taking so long for her to open the door.

The problem, for me, was when the door finally came open, she was standing there with a big pistol in her hands. "Is Pops here?" I asked, hoping she wouldn't answer with a bullet to my head. "Pops don't live here anymore, and who are you anyway?" she replied. I told her my name again and that I was a friend of his, but she just stood there in the doorway staring at me. I went on, explaining how I'd met Pops through my older brother Demetrice back in the mid-eighties. She relaxed, and invited me in, offering me a seat on the couch. I sat down. I was tired. So tired that if she told me to sit on the floor, I would have.

She said that Pops had moved to California several years before. I asked for his address but she wouldn't give it to me, offering to call him instead. When she got him on the line she said, "Demetrice's brother's over here and wants to talk to you." Then she handed me the phone.

I could tell she wanted me out of her house so I didn't waste time telling Pops why I was looking for him. I told him I needed to get out of town, like yesterday. "What's the hurry? Are you in some kind of trouble?" he asked. "I don't want to talk about it over the phone," I said. He asked if I needed a bus ticket and I told him I didn't, but needed his address. He gave it to me and I told him I'd call when I got there. I hung up the phone, thanked the woman, got up and walked out the door, on my way to the bus station.

My trip to California took longer than it should have, and it was all my fault. I purchased the wrong ticket, thinking Oakland was part of the city of Los Angeles. When I got to Los Angeles, I hailed a cab and gave the driver the address Pops had given to me. He looked at me and asked if I was sure that I had enough money to pay the fare. I told him I did. He looked at me a few seconds more, then said I'd caught the wrong bus and I was hundreds of miles from Oakland. I thanked him, got out of the cab, and went to the ticket counter. I told the woman behind it what had happened and she laughed, but nevertheless, gave me a ticket to Oakland. The bus arrived in Oakland a day later and by that time I was wide awake because I'd slept most of the trip. I was nervous because I knew the police in St. Louis was looking for me by then, even though I didn't think they knew where I was. I stayed in my seat until the other passengers got off the bus, looking out the window for any signs of the police. I sat there a while, thinking. I didn't know a thing about Oakland - not how many people lived there, if the city had alleys – nothing. But one thing I did know was I couldn't sit there forever.

I got off the bus and the first thing I noticed was how warm it was outside. It was well over seventy degrees. A real shocker because the city I'd just left was freezing cold with snow on the ground. I stood in front of a small building I figured was the bus station because people were going in and out if it. I wasn't going to go inside but changed my mind. I figured if the police were waiting, I'd have a better chance of escaping with all the people milling around. Yeah, I know. It was a stupid idea but I never claimed to be a genius!

I was going inside but first had to call Pops to let him know I was there. I walked over to a pay phone outside the station and dialed his number. He didn't answer so I waited a minute, then dialed again. Still no answer. I hung up the phone and looked around downtown Oakland. I walked into the station but it wasn't what I'd expected. The place was small and raggedy, dirty, too. There was a row of plastic chairs, a vending machine that didn't work, a restroom and a ticket counter. That was it. I walked out and down the street, not knowing where I was going.

Downtown Oakland looked more like Times Square than anything. People were walking back and forth, bumping into each other, not saying excuse me. Every building I passed looked ready to collapse, including the Wells Fargo bank. It was a stark contrast to downtown St. Louis. There, you never saw a piece of paper on the ground. That's why the police kept the gang bangers from going there, and if they did, they'd be sitting in jail looking at prison time.

I walked around sightseeing for a couple of hours before realizing I was lost, and had to stop a woman on the sidewalk and ask for directions to a pay phone. She told me there was one around the corner. I thanked her then went to call Pops again. He picked up this time and I told him where I was so he could come pick me up. He said he'd be there in a minute, so I hung up.

I stood on the corner waiting for a while before he pulled along the curb in the smallest car I'd ever seen. But what really took me back was the sight of him getting out of it – all 300 pounds of him! He was huge. Much bigger than he was the last time I saw him back in 1987. He bear hugged me and I put my arms around as much of him as I could. I noticed he wore a blue security uniform so I asked him about it. He said he'd tricked a security firm into hiring him. I use the word "tricked" because I knew what kind of person lie under that uniform. Pops was as crooked as two left shoes. He's the only person I knew who had committed more burglaries than me. But the difference was he was smart enough to wear gloves and I wasn't.

So there I was, cruising around a big city, in a little car driven by a big dude with little cornrows in his hair. We talked for a while about old times, then he started asking me about what it was like being in prison. That was the last thing I wanted to talk about but I did share a few things with him. Afterwards he asked if I wanted to get high. I told him I was cool but could use a little money since I'd spent most of what Vanita had given me. He reached into his pocket, pulled out a roll of bills and peeled off a couple – giving me $200. I sat there thinking. I wanted to get high real bad, as if he knew what I was thinking, so he pulled into an alley and took a some crack and a pipe out of his pocket. He looked over at me and said, "Sure you don't want to get high?" I started sweating.

We got high. Afterwards he dropped me off at a shelter on 73rd & East 14th Street. He said I could stay there during the day but when it got dark, I had to go to a different shelter that provided beds for homeless people to sleep at night. I could tell when I first walked in that the shelter used to be a diner. On one side of the room was a counter and on the other side was a few tables. The floor was made of old rotting wood and the walls were steel with no paint on them. They gave away free cups of coffee if you asked for it, and I did, but before I finished drinking it, a loud bell rang signaling closing time.

I reached down, grabbed my bag of clothes from the floor, and walked outside to a warm spring night. I turned left and started walking the short distance to the other shelter Pops had told me about. I could tell I was in the ghetto. There's no mistaking a place like that. Some people can tell if they're in the ghetto by the large number of black people walking around, or the large amount of drugs being sold. But that can be deceiving. There's a better way of knowing if you're in the ghetto as there's a liquor store and a church on every corner.

When I arrived at the shelter, I was told I couldn't stay without providing a picture ID. They also said they'd have to run a police check on me. As soon as they said that, I was out of there! I walked around the corner to call Pops on a pay phone. His girlfriend Wanda answered and said he was asleep. I asked if she'd wake him up but she refused. I could tell by the sound of her voice that she was angry and that her anger was directed at me. I couldn't figure out why because I had never met her. Maybe I woke her up or something, I don't know. I went on, explaining the situation and who I was. Pops had told her…confessed is more like it. But she hung up on me. Come to find out he went home to her high as a kite and blamed it all on me!

I still had the pipe Pops left with me and there were a couple hits still inside it that I planned on saving until the next day. But after being turned away from the shelter, not being able to contact Pops, I figured on finding an alley or vacant house so I could get high. I walked several blocks looking for the right spot and eventually picked a vacant house. I stood across the street in the shadow watching it. It was painted bright blue and all the windows were missing. That is usually a sign that nobody was inside. No addict wanted to get high in a house missing its windows. Too spooky!

I walked across the street and went inside, stopping in the foyer. I wasn't going any further than that. I took the pipe out of my pocket, put the flame to it, and inhaled deeply. The inmates in prison used to say California had the best dope this side of the Mississippi. I didn't know what side the Mississippi was on but whatever side, the hit I took made me have to sit on the floor to keep from falling over. I can't remember taking the second one, all I remember was me waking up the next morning on the floor with the lighter and pipe beside my face, just as I found my mother barely a week ago. I got up, left the house to look for a pay phone so I could call Pops.

"You're welcome to come in and sit, if you would like, young man." I turned and saw the voice belonging to an elderly black man. "Are you talking to me?" I asked. He smiled and said, "You're the only one out here, aren't you?" My back was sore. Pops and I had been sitting up for days getting high. "I'm cool," I told the old man, standing up to try to work out the kinks in my back. I had to get out of there. I don't know what I was thinking, falling asleep at a church. "I used to be just like you, young man," the man went on. "Running. Always running from somebody you can't escape from. You know what that somebody was? It was the Lord. No matter how far you run, or where you hide, He'll always be there." I started walking down the street. "God bless you!" I heard behind me.

"God?" I thought. "What has your honky God done for me? For anybody?! Nothing, that's what!!" I was tired of hearing people talking about the Lord and His stupid plans. If He did have a plan for me, it wasn't about nothing. Where was His stupid plan when Preacher got gunned down in the street, or when Diane was burning to death in a fire? Where was He and His stupid plan then?

I found a pay phone and called Pops but he didn't answer so I walked over to his house on MacArthur & High Street. I was broke, dirty and hungry. I couldn't remember the last time I had something to eat. On my way there, I stopped at KFC for a free glass of water. I thought about asking the woman behind the counter for a free piece of chicken but changed my mind. I didn't like begging people, especially those stringy haired white folks.

I got to Pops' house and rang the doorbell. Wanda opened the door and invited me in. I sat down on the couch and looked at her. She was skinny. Too skinny. Pops had told me she used to get high but had stopped. Looking at her, I didn't believe that for a minute. I hadn't been getting high all that long but long enough to know a fellow addict when I saw one. I saw one in Wanda. I smelled it and saw it written on her dry, sunken face. Her hair was even nappier than mine! When Pops walked into the room, I stood and told him I needed to talk to him outside. We talked for a while and it wasn't long before we started talking about drugs and how we could get high. Neither of us had any money to buy anything but he told me there was a guy he knew who owed him money and I could go with him to pick it up if I liked. I agreed but said I was starving. He went in the house, came back with two cheese sandwiches and I ate them on the way to his friend's house.

There's always a sign that screams, "This stinks!" but we rarely pay attention until it's too late, when we finding ourselves wishing we had. Of course, by then it's too late. That day was one of those times. I asked Pops why we had to walk such a long distance to his friend's house when we could get there quicker in his car but he never answered my question. I should've known then that something was terribly wrong. I did feel something but wanted to get high so bad I ignored it. There were times in my life I wished I would've paid more attention to that small voice in my head that warned me of danger. It may have saved somebody's life.

I stood on the sidewalk waiting on Pops who had been in the house for over twenty minutes. We were in a neighborhood I'd never been in and it looked to be upper middle class. The lawns were neat and I didn't notice any trash scattered about, it reminded me of when we lived in University City. I knew the look. We were in the white people's neighborhood and that made me nervous. What if one of them looked out their window and saw my black nappy head, standing there looking suspicious? That did it for me. I started walking up the steps.

When I got to the porch, I heard a loud yell and something or someone crashing to the floor. I rushed through the door, finding myself in the living room, and Pops on top of somebody, hitting them in the face. I walked around to where they were tussling on the floor and then I saw it…the Phillip's head screwdriver Pops had in his hand. I saw the blood, too, a lot of it on him and the guy he was stabbing. Pops plunged the screwdriver over and over into the guy's face, neck and chest. I yelled for him to stop but either he didn't hear me or chose to ignore me. I reached down, grabbed him by the jacket, and pulled with all my might until we fell backwards onto the floor. I could see the whole scene then. The man he stabbed was oozing blood and it was everywhere. And he was dead.

I picked myself up off the floor and ran out of the house, stopping on the sidewalk, trying to figure out which way to run. Pops came out and started off down the street so I took off behind him, watching as he took items out of his pockets and threw them to the ground. That's when I knew what the fight was about – robbery. We ran on until we reached an intersection. Across the street was a parked named Lake Merrit. I looked at Pops and noticed blood all over his jacket and that made me look down at my own. There was blood on it, too, so I took it off and tossed it into the entrance of the building behind me.

Pops said we'd have a better chance of getting away if we split up. That was music to my ears because I wanted to get as far away from him as I could. He took off in one direction and I walked across the street and into the park. I figured since there were a lot of people there, it'd be harder for the police to single me out. I was sweating, feeling like I would pass out. I saw a water fountain and stopped to have a drink and to wash the blood off of my shoes. Afterwards I walked to the other side of the part to East 14th Street.

There, I turned around and looked behind me to see if anybody was watching. I noticed people walking and jogging but nobody paying attention to me. I thought about going to Pops' house to pick up what little clothes I had there but ruled that out, figuring it wasn't worth the risk. What if the police were there waiting? What would I tell them? Whatever I said, I knew they wouldn't believe me. Forget the clothes, I was leaving town. I turned right and started the longest walk of my life. Seventy long blocks down East 14th Street and several more to a truck stop. When I walked into the diner, white people were looking at me like they'd never seen a black man before. I felt compelled to have a stare-down with a fat, overall-wearing with a cowboy hat on his head white man until he averted his eyes. I took a seat at a table, ordered pancakes and eggs, without giving a thought about how I was going to pay for it.

CHAPTER 12: TAKOMA, WASHINGTON

"And not many days after the younger son gathered
all together, and took his journey into the far country,
and there wasted his substance with riotous
living." – Luke 15:13

"Living it up in the Hotel California, such a lovely place." I sat at the
table wondering who picked that stupid song? I'd been living in
California for several weeks and found nothing "lovely" about it. I sure
as heck wasn't "living it up" either! It wasn't until I finished eating that I
realized I didn't have money to pay the bill. I looked around the diner,
noticing it was packed with truck drivers. Most of them white, too. The
pretty waitress who took my order never came back to my table so I got
up and walked out of the door.

There were dozens of semi's sitting in the parking lot and I thought
about stealing one but the problem was that I didn't know how. Even if I
could've gotten one started, I didn't know how to shift the gears. I saw a
slim black man getting out of a truck. I stood by a wooden telephone
pole and looked him over. He didn't look like a truck driver to me.
"Maybe he hitched a ride," I thought. I walked over and told him I was
on the run and needed out of Oakland as quick as possible and did he
know where I could go? He told me his name was Kenny and he didn't
know where I could hide from the law but would love to give me a lift up
north if I'd let him say a prayer for me. I looked at the truck he got out
of. It was bright orange with the name "Digby" painted in white. I was
surprised that he was a truck driver because I thought trucking

companies only hired white people.

He bowed his head and started praying. The first words out of his mouth were, "Lord Jesus," and I wanted to kill him right there. While he prayed, I stared at the top of his head, wishing I could put a bullet in it. I was so mad, tears rolled down my face. "Imma kill this nigga," I thought. "Praying to that honky God to help me with something? Imma kill this nigga!" When he finished praying, we hopped into his truck and I watching him go about flipping switches, pushing buttons and preparing to start the engine. He was bone thin, not weighing more than 130 pounds. I was certain I could overpower him. "Yeah, this nigga is dead," I thought. I looked around the cabin for something I could steal and sell for crack but the only thing I saw was a CB radio and it was screwed into the dash. But I knew Kenny had to have some money on him and I planned to get it, then kill him.

We drove along I-5 for a couple of hours, with him talking the whole time. I found out that he lived in Los Angeles and was married to a "woman of God." I asked him why he drove trucks for a living and he said it gave him the opportunity to "be alone with the Lord." I was content letting him talk about God and Jesus, until he started with that "Jesus has a plan for you" crap. That's when the "debater in chief" came roaring out. I countered everything he said about God and Jesus with something I'd read in the Qur'an. I tried everything, hit him with everything I had, but couldn't get under his skin. I got so upset I started cursing him and Jesus out, calling them every foul and disgusting name I could think of. I told him Christianity was a "white devil religion, designed to keep the black man down." I went at him the whole two and a half days it took us to reach Tacoma, Washington, where he was to drop off his load. I was so mad and caught up on trying to prove him wrong that it wasn't until he dropped me off at the "Pink Elephant" that I remembered, "Damn, I forgot to kill that nigga!"

So there I was, walking the streets in the middle of the night, in a city I'd never heard of. No money, no friends, no luck. I had to find somewhere to sleep because it was raining hard and the streets were deserted. For somebody trying to avoid the police, that was bad news. Walking the streets late at night was a sure fire way to get their attention. I saw lights a couple of blocks up ahead so I started walking towards them. When I got there, I looked at the street sign – 25the & Pacific. Now what? Left? Right? If I went left, I'd be headed over a bridge, the one that punk Kenny drove over into the city. There was no other way to go but down Pacific.

It was a long street, stretching as far as the eye could see. There were businesses on both sides but I couldn't make out what they were because the rain was coming down so hard. It wouldn't have mattered anyway because I didn't have any money. I started walking and after a few blocks, ran into a homeless guy who told me about a shelter just a couple blocks away from where I was, where I could get something to eat and a bed for the night. I followed the directions he gave me but when I got there, it was closed until the following morning. I'd missed the deadline.

Weeks later I was in a vacant house, crawling on my hands and knees, searching the floor to see if I'd dropped any crumbs of crack. I was sweating and my heart was racing. I'd been getting high by myself for days. I like it that was because I hated sharing. The only time I'd share was if I had to or when I was spooked. Crack did that. It spooked you. Made you think somebody or something was lurking behind every car, every building, every shadow. There would always places that made you think the police were around as you could hear their walkie talkies. I brought my hands to my face, looking under my nails for crumbs. No luck there. The house looked like all the others I'd been in, walls with holes in them, windows missing, no doors and old furniture scattered everywhere. And they all smelled like mildew. I got up and went to the window and looked out to the street, trying to remember where I was. I knew I was in Tacoma but just didn't know what part. I put my hands in my pockets, searching for money, but they were empty. I needed to get high because I was sick. I could feel the old .38 revolver I had tucked in my waist.

I left the house and started walking towards the shelter to get something to eat. When I got there, I grabbed a couple of sandwiches and a glass of milk, then went to an empty table in the corner and sat down to eat. The shelter was in a building that used to be a warehouse and it was always packed with people just like me – addicts. I looked around for a familiar face. I'd gotten high a few times with some of the people who stayed there from time to time but I didn't recognize any of them in the crowd. I was going through withdrawals and was looking for someone to help me burglarize a house. If I didn't get high soon, I'd go crazy. Maybe I was already crazy?

One day I was waiting in a long line at a temp service, searching for a job. I was looking for a job because I needed money to buy dope. I'd been living with Margaret-Ann Steves in a three bedroom apartment on 9th Street for a couple of weeks. I met her one day while I was walking around her neighborhood, looking for something to steal. It had been raining and I was getting soaked. She was standing on her porch while I walked by and asked me if I wanted to join her there until it stopped raining. She offered me a beer, which I turned down.

We sat on the porch and talked for a while. Margaret-Ann was in her early thirties and had three small children, a girl and two boys. Her hair was long and wavy and she stood 5'6" tall, with light brown skin. When she asked me what my name was, I lied, telling her it was Timothy. The reason I gave her my brother's name was because he'd never been in trouble with the law, in case she ran a check on me it would come back clean. She seemed like a cool person but I couldn't afford to take any chances. After I gave her the fake name, she asked what city I was from? I lied again, telling her I was from Chicago. I think she knew I was lying.

"Do you have ID, sir?" the woman at the counter asked. I looked across the counter at her. She was white. I'd stood in line for over an hour to apply for a job and my legs were hurting. "No ma'am, I just got in from Chicago the other day and I lost my wallet on the bus," I replied. "Well, you can't work without an ID," she said. I looked down at her. She looked like the housekeeper on the television show *Different Strokes*. I told her I needed a job real bad and if I didn't find one soon, I'd be forced to live on the streets. "Let's pray about it," she said. I told her, "Look lady, I don't need you or anybody else praying to no white man's God for me."

"Do you want a job or what?" she countered. I really wanted to knock her head off but I stood there while she prayed the same stupid prayer – Jesus dying for my sins – in Him I'm a new creature. What's wrong with these people? Everybody I meet wants to pray for me!

After she finished 'praying for my soul,' she told me to have a seat in the waiting area and "we'll see what happens." I did what she said but I was mad as hell. I couldn't stand hearing those stupid prayers! I tried calming myself down by grabbing a magazine off the table and reading it. A few minutes passed and she came back saying a job had just came in. "See, I told you the Lord would provide," she said. I said, "I hear you." I really wanted to curse her out but knew doing so wouldn't be wise.

My job assignment was working on a farm for a white man named John Percinich, just about twenty miles from Tacoma in Gig Harbor. The "100X" was the only bus that went to Gig Harbor and the women at the temp service had given me some tokens for fare. I worked for John for a little over two weeks and hated it. Not working for him but the bus ride itself because it crossed a long bridge somebody told me fell into Puget

Sound in the mid-1900s. I heard the only loss of life was a dog.

John was a middle aged man and was married to a white woman named Nancy. They had two adult children who were away at college. The farm was a ten acre spread with two houses and an apartment on it. I painted the inside of the apartment the first day on the job and enjoyed every minute of it because I was working alone. I hated working with people, plus Johnny paid me $80 a day regardless of how much work I accomplished. John was a nice man and I tried to hate him. He was all the things I despised – white, rich and Christian. "You have a story to tell," he'd say to me every day. He said it so much, I got used to hearing it and paid him no mind. I'm almost certain he lifted my fingerprints and had them run through the computer by a police buddy of his because one day we were working together and he leaned over and said, "I know all about you Timothy."

I stayed in Tacoma a couple of months but I was homesick, wanting to see my family, especially my daughter MeMe. I talked to John and Nancy about it and they put a few hundred dollars together for me to purchase a bus ticket back to St. Louis. After buying the ticket, I had enough money left to get two $50 rocks. I smoked as much as I could on the day I was to leave because I didn't want to get caught with it on the bus. But I did have a few crumbs left when I boarded and I went to the bathroom and smoked them. It was a three day drive to St. Louis and without something to get high off of, I was sick the whole time.

CHAPTER 13: BACK HOME (1994)

"But he that hateth his brother is in darkness,
and walketh in darkness, and knoweth not
whither he goeth, because that darkness hath
blinded his eyes." – I John 2:11

I decided to walk to my mother's house. I enjoyed taking long walks through the city, especially with Diane. It just seemed as if you saw and appreciated what you saw more when you were walking instead of riding in a car. I was walking for only a few minutes before I ran into a guy named Mike. I didn't know him but could tell he was an addict and was going through withdrawals, too. His clothes were old and dirty, hair nappy and his shoes had holes in them. It was easy to see. Long story short, we broke into a house, stole some jewelry and took it to a drug dealer who traded it for crack. After that, we went to a vacant house and got high.

I was alone when I woke up. Mike was gone and I never saw him again. I was so messed up I didn't even know where I was until I walked outside. "I've got to go see Momma," I thought. Regardless of her shortcomings, I loved my mother and missed her dearly. She couldn't give me the life I thought I deserved but every time we were apart, my heard would bleed love.

I knocked on the door. "Who is it?" came the voice of a child. "It's Uncle Tony," I said. The voice belonged to my niece ReRe, a cute three-year-old. She opened the door and I reached down and gave her a hug. "Uncle Tony, the police keeps coming here looking for you," she said. I told her not to worry, that I wasn't in any trouble. I said it with a calmness I didn't feel. But I was worried because when I was in Tacoma, I called home and my mother told me I was on *Crime Stoppers*. Everybody on there got caught. At least everybody I'd met in prison.

I figured on seeing my mother, then leaving. We sat on the couch talking for a while, with ReRe on the floor watching cartoons. I started crying when my mother said she was going to the kitchen to fix me something to eat. I remember thinking, "Why does this keep happening to me? I'm stronger than this. I'm a Black Muslim. I'm stronger than this, aren't I?"

We talked a little more after we ate. ReRe was a lively little girl, very energetic, and I thought about staying longer just to play with her, but I knew I had to leave. I took a shower, then put on one of Tim's outfits he had left there. My mother asked if I'd stop by before I left town again and I said I would. I gave them a kiss before walking out the door on my way to Danielle's house.

She lived a couple neighborhoods over from my mother and like all the other neighborhood's in the city, it was run down but it used to be a beautiful place to live, back when white people lived there. North St. Louis was predominantly black but it used to be the opposite. When a few black families moved in, the white people moved out.

No one answered when I knocked on the door so I walked around back and found Danielle sitting in a lawn chair drinking a beer. I walked over, grabbed a beer out of the cooler, and sat across from her. She hadn't changed much over the years. A beautiful woman with a chubby face that always wore a smile. She wasn't smiling that day. She was sad, I could tell. Demetrice and her had been an item once and they had several children together. I asked about their kids.

She said they were fine but one had died. It was a girl. She told me people were saying she'd got high and killed her baby. "Do you think I'd do something like that, Tony?" she asked. "No, I know you wouldn't," I said. And I did know. She may have been a lot of things but she'd never harm a child. I sat there, listening to her talk for a while, just letting her have her moment. Then got around to why I'd came to see her – my daughter.

Danielle told me the gifts I'd sent MeMe while I was in prison had never got to her. Not with my name on them, at least. She said Minica scratched my name off of them and replaced it with hers, making it look like they'd come from her. The more she talked, the more upset I became. Monica told MeMe I was a murderer and didn't care about her. I had never killed anyone before but made up my mind that day, I was going to kill Monica. I gave Danielle a hug and left her sitting there in her back yard.

I was going to see Jerome Hill, who by that time was one of the biggest drug dealers in St. Louis. He owned houses in the city and county, and a parking lot downtown where he charged white people an arm and a leg to park their cars on. Jerome had a gang of drugs but I never asked for any because I knew he'd never give me none.

"Tony, what you tripping off man?!" he said. We were standing on his front porch and I just asked him for a gun so I could kill Monica. Even through my ears, I saw the concerned look on his face. "You can't kill your baby Momma, dog," he went on. "Imma kill that bitch!" I yelled. The reason I went to him for a gun was I knew he wouldn't call the police on me. I tried changing his mind but after a while, I realized I was wasting my time. I gave up, told him I'd catch him later, then left for my mother's house. I walked slow because I needed time to think. When I finally got there, I ate and went to bed. The next day would be Tim's birthday, June 13th.

The next morning, I woke feeling something cold on my face. It was a beer. I looked up and Tim was smiling down at me. "Get up Tony, man. I've got to make a quick run but when I get back, we gonna kick it for my birthday!" he said. "Okay," I mumbled, then rolled back over on the couch where I'd been sleeping. I was still tired so I went back to sleep. I was woke up again feeling something cold on my face. But this time it wasn't Tim and his cold beer. It was the cold barrel of a policeman's Glock 9mm handgun.

CHAPTER 14: PRISON, AGAIN

"Then shall they also answer him saying, Lord when
saw we thee an hungered, or athirst, or stranger, or
naked, or sick, or in prison, and did not minister unto
thee? Then shall be he answer them, saying, verily I say
unto you, Inasmuch as ye did it not to one of the
least of these, ye did it not to me." – Matt. 25:44-45

Some people say all police are good police, that they can do no
wrong. They hear the stories – police killing young black men – and they
say, "He just have done something wrong." Even after a video proves
them wrong, the police are always right, so says these kinds of people.
And these kinds of people are, almost all of the time, white people. They
believe everything they see on the news. Blacks commit more crimes than
whites, let them tell it. Most drug dealers and addicts are black, so says
these kinds of people. There's no 'innocent until proven guilty' for black
people. We are 'guilty until proven innocent', and even then, we were
guilty. The year was 1994.

I was innocent, 'and' guilty. Innocent of stealing the car, guilty of
traffic violations. Well, I did violate parole by leaving town without
permission, so I guess I'm guilty of that, too. I was faced with a choice –
plead guilty or stand trial. I didn't have any money for a personal attorney
and if I went to trial with a public defender, I'd die behind bars. That's
how they did it in St. Louis back then, and how they do it now...if you're
black.

The guy who Lisa had rented the car from admitted he stole it during the home invasion and rented it to us without our knowledge of a crime, but the prosecutor refused to drop the charges. That was the reality for young black men in 1994. Most white people didn't care what happened to us, as long as 'them people' were kept in the cities, away from them and their families because rural America was safe. But they had no idea the difference twenty years would make, when Mr. and Mrs. Opioid came knocking on their front door. They didn't have a clue that, twenty years later, it would be their children in those court rooms, shackled to 'them people,' being sentenced to years in prison alongside 'them people.' They had no idea. Not back then.

I had no idea how much a hateful person I was. Not back then. I had no idea how much pain and heartache I'd brought upon myself. I wish that I'd known Jesus back then. It would've been so much easier for me, for everyone. But I didn't know Jesus and it was easy for no one who crossed my path. I was such an angry person. And that's why I was standing in the shower at Farmington Correctional Center washing blood off of me. There was a five gallon bucket full of bleach water that I was using to scrub the blood out of my clothes and to remove any traces of DNA. I was in a rush because I knew it wouldn't be long before the officers would come for me. They would come for twelve of us, all Black Muslims, who had just got into a big fight on the prison yard.

I stepped out of the shower, went to my cell, and put on some clean clothes. When that was done, I walked over to the window and looked out at the yard where the incident took place. Nurses were everywhere, tending to the wounded inmates laying all over the yard. I looked to see if I saw our leader, Minister Herbert X but he was nowhere in sight. He had got away. Turning from the window, I lit a Kool cigarette and smoked it, then another, until I heard the sallyport door open and close. "Here them honkies come," I thought.

When the cell door opened, a half dozen officers rushed in, wrestling me to the ground. Handcuffs were slapped on my wrists and I was carted off to administrative segregation where, an hour later, I was issued a conduct violation for 'organized disobedience' and 'assault.' Herbert X never got caught but was transferred to the other side of the prison and so I became the leader of every Muslim on the side I was on. I had only been back to prison two weeks and I was already in trouble.

I was sentenced to serve a year in the hole but I kept in touch with associates by passing kites back and forth. I thought I had everything figured out because I spent the whole year plotting and planning. I had only two days before I'd be released to general population and I couldn't wait! I missed being a leader. Second in command was cool but top-dog was better because I answered to no one. I hated Christians. Hated seeing them in the yard preaching about God and Jesus. I pace the floor until my feet got sore.

The next day I did the same thing, paced the floor, anxiously waiting to get out so I could kill one of those 'white devils.' The closer it got to 9 o'clock a.m., the faster my heart beat. When the officer finally came and opened my cell door, I knew something was wrong but I couldn't put my and on it. Was it his body language? His eyes? I had an uneasy feeling in the pit of my stomach that I should've paid attention to, but I didn't. I which I had.

The prison's largest gangs were the crips and bloods. Every single one of them were black. Then there were the up and coming white gangs who hated blacks, especially the Black Muslims. Without leadership, the Muslims had grown weak and disorganized. The white inmates saw their weakness and pounced, organizing gangs of their own. They couldn't have done that if the black gangs had remained unified. But they hadn't. The white gangs tricked them, giving them drugs. They passed it out like candy. A few months later, the white gangs took over the prison. When all of this was going on, nobody told me anything. Maybe they didn't realize what was happening or maybe they did and just didn't tell me.

"What you don't know won't hurt you," we were taught as kids. That was a lie. I didn't know that when I walked out of the hole that people were waiting to kill me but I did get hurt. I wound up in the hospital, busted up, stitches all over my body. And the scary part about the whole thing was I didn't know what had happened. I found out some white inmates caught me coming out the door, snuck up and busted my head with a pipe, and stabbed me several times. It was a white doctor who told me, "The Lord was with you, Anthony."

CHAPTER 15: THE RUNNING MAN

"For man also knoweth not his time: as the
fishes that are taken in an evil net, and
as the birds that are caught in the snare;
so are the sons of men snared in an evil
time, when it falleth suddenly upon them." – Eccl. 9:12

There comes a time when 'I didn't know' doesn't work anymore. It does when we're kids but not so much when we're adults. I knew right from wrong as a child, but knowing right from wrong was useless without Christ in my life. Success is impossible without the guidance of the Holy Spirit because real and true success lies I Christ, and without Him, we're all failures. That man at the church in Oakland was right. I was running. Running from God. But I didn't know it. I know that sounds ridiculous but it's true. I never knew God and without knowing Him, it was impossible to know His/my adversary – Satan. We can't know one without knowing the other because the revelation of one is the revelation of both.

I didn't use Stan's hand in my affairs and as a result, I couldn't fight an enemy I didn't see. For me, Satan (aka the devil) was white people. Nobody can fight an enemy they have no knowledge of. Hosea 4:6 says, "My people are destroyed for lack of knowledge." This is talking about the knowledge of Christ, not of this world. We have satellites capable of seeing galaxies light years away, still many of us are blind to the glorious gospel of Jesus Christ. I know, because I was one of them. That old man was right, there's no running from God.

"Dear Tony, your dad died, sorry." That was it. A few words on a small piece of paper. I sat on my bunk, looking out the window at the two-lane highway bordering the prison. Just a few words from my mother, who I hadn't seen in years. I was in the hole for trying to escape from the dentist's office in Festus, Missouri, where I was getting my wisdom tooth pulled. I jumped an officer and took off in an ambulance. That happened on November 22, 2004, and I heard it was on the news. I had no way of knowing if that was true or not, since we weren't allowed televisions in the hole. At least not in the year 2005, the year after my father died.

But I didn't cry. Didn't shed one single tear. I turned from the window, wondering if my daughter would cry when I died. She probably wouldn't, and I wouldn't expect her to since she didn't know me. I didn't know my father, but over the years had ran into inmates who said they did. They said the same thing about him as people was saying about me – that he was crazy. I'd been at Southeast Correctional Center (SECC) since February 2004. It was a new prison but looking at it, you'd never know. The ceilings were cracked, toilets leaked and there wasn't any sealing around the windows.

I sat back on my bunk and listened to the silence. I used to hate it but then I welcomed it. I was thirty-four-years-old, and felt like it. That wasn't my first escape attempt. I tried when I was at FCC in May of 2002. The courts gave me a white public defender named Jolene Taafe. I had since forgot about that escape but was reminded of it when I received a letter from her notifying me of her appointment as my counsel. Her letter took me back to how it all went down. Really wasn't much to it. "Prisoner #163116" had no plans to serve his 22 year prison term, so "Prisoner #163116" made a break for it one night and was caught on the rooftop.

I was immediately charged with 'attempted escape' but the courts didn't pursue the case until 2005, and the only reason they did then was because a prosecutor saw me on television in cuffs for the 2004 attempt. Wendy Wexler, the head prosecutor at the time, had forgot to prosecute me. That was good news for me because by the time my case was to go to trial (June 2006), the three year statute of limitations had ran out. My attorney filed a motion to dismiss and the judge granted it.

SECC is a maximum security prison that sits in the city of Charleston, Missouri. It was built to house inmates serving life sentences without parole but due to increase in Missouri's prison population, inmates were housed in any prison the state had an open bed. It didn't matter how much time you had, you could easily find yourself where I was in 2005 – the hole. Walter Mountain was one such inmate and he'd been there two years before me. He and another inmate named Buddha had got drunk off of some homemade wine, grabbed a shank and carved their names in an inmate's forehead. They got five years in the hole for that.

Buddha was downstairs and Walter was in a cell across the hall from where I was. He's the one who gave me the cigarette I lit up. I took a long drag. Yep, the pain was still there in my lower abdomen. It started a week before and I thought it was from me exercising and overdoing it. I didn't notify medical at the time but became concerned because it didn't go away. It wasn't just the pain in my abdomen that was bothering me, I was also having problems with urination too often, and sometimes not at all. I knew something was terribly wrong with me but I still refused to see a doctor. Instead, I chose to ignore it. I was running.

CHAPTER 16: NOWHERE TO RUN

"And when he cometh home, he calleth together
his friends and neighbors, saying unto them,
Rejoice with me; for I have found my sheep
which was lost." – Luke 15:6

MSP was closed, the only sign it was over there was the 'Death House,' the inmates were executed, gassed in a steel chamber resembling a small space capsule. I saw it every day that I was there. It was a gray building made of huge concrete blocks. There were no windows. It still sits there to this very day, and you can go see for yourself if you'd like but you won't be able to see inside it since it didn't have any widows.

The Jefferson City Correctional Center (JCCC) sits on 25 acres in Jefferson City, Missouri, and houses over 3,000 inmates serving life without parole or its equivalent. To this day, I can't figure out why I was sent there, with me serving just 22 years, but not as much as I used to. I didn't have the energy.

"Are you okay Mr. Cook?" asked Dr. Swartz. We were sitting in a small room in the prison's medical unit. I didn't know how to respond to her question so I remained quiet until she got up and left the room. I looked around but there wasn't much to see, just a steel table and two metal chairs. Dr. Swartz returned a while later with an older white man beside her. This was a man I hated the site o, but in the coming months I would grow to love him dearly. His name was Dr. Darrin.

When he tried introducing himself, I didn't give him a chance. Instead, I cursed him and Dr. Swartz out. I went off so bad to where the officers had to come drag me back to my cell, me fighting them the whole way. They removed the handcuffs through the food port and I walked over to the sink, splashing water on my face. Afterwards, I stood there with my head lowered for a minute, watching the tears drip and land on the steel sink. I can't say how long I cried but eventually I raised my head, looked into the mirror and prayed, "Oh Allah, how could you do this to me? What have I done to deserve this punishment? I've served you night and day until my lungs were about to bust. What have I done?" When I got no answer, I sat down on my bunk, not believing what Dr. Swartz had told me...I had prostate cancer.

"There must be some kind of mistake," I thought. "Allah wouldn't let me die this way. I've served him well. I'd beat and stabbed Christians in his name, even tried to kill a few." I walked back to the sink and looked into the mirror again, not recognizing the person staring back at me. I did see something, though. I saw all the ugly things I'd done and the people I'd hurt throughout my life. I saw the beatings, stabbings and shootings. That day, when I looked in the mirror, I saw a monster.

The year was 2011 and I'd been at JCCC for four years and had eleven more to serve before my release. That's what the judge had said but prostate cancer said otherwise. I started praying day and night for Allah to heal me, for forgiveness, for mercy. I was so ashamed because I'd failed at everything and everyone. Time in the hole started slipping away and I dropped from 185 pounds to 115 pounds. Cancer spread from my anal area to my stomach and no matter how much I ate it wouldn't stay down. I received every treatment available but nothing worked. The cancer continued to spread. Dr. Swartz read and took my vitals daily, giving me pills for pain. The pain intensified. I was dying. I thought about my mother. What would I tell her? Nothing. I would tell her nothing. I didn't want to live anymore and decided to commit suicide.

For me, self-disgust was the turning point in my live. Every time I looked into the mirror, I saw it. Whenever I'd have memories of the past, it was there. There was no getting away from it as it was everywhere I looked. I realized my plan for living wasn't working. I'd hit rock bottom. Satan controlled me, made me a killer, I was his slave. Drug addiction gutted me and destroyed every dream I had. It put stitches on my body and bullets in my chest. Made me raggedy as a bowl of sauerkraut. Drug addiction took me to a place I never thought I'd be. Robbing, stealing, living in the streets, eating out of garbage cans and selling the shoes on my feet. I wasn't alone. There were others like me. I'd seen them in the alleys, hear gunshots and they're gone. I was scared.

I took a bed sheet off my bunk, tore it into strips with one end around my neck and the other around the rail. I jumped. Then there came silence and I just knew it meant I was dead. But I wasn't. I was alive and in pain. My head was throbbing and my whole body hurting. I was in more pain than when I jumped over the rail. Slowly I opened my eyes and saw I was in a Suicide Observation cell. Another failure. I remember laying on the floor thinking, "I'm so dumb I can't even kill myself." I sat up and looked around but there wasn't much to see. The cell was padded with no fixtures, not even a mirror. That was somewhat comforting because I could only imagine what I looked like. There was a toilet, if you can call it that. It was basically a hole in the middle of the cell. I had a job at another prison cleaning cells like the one I was in. Back then, I thought anybody who tried to kill themselves was crazy and I made it a point of telling them so. I sat there wondering what they would think of me if they saw me sitting there in that paper gown.

I was hungry so I looked around the cell for the brown paper bag of sandwiches inmates were given three times a day while in the Suicide Observation cells. I wasn't wearing my glasses so I had a difficult time locating it. I spotted something in the corner and went over and picked it up. It was smooth and hard, definitely not a bag. It was a book and not just any book, either. It was the Holy Bible.

I tossed it across the room where it bounced off the padding and landed on the floor with a thud. I was hot! So much so that I ran to the door, started kicking it and threatening whoever was on the other side of it. I figured they'd put the Bible in there because I was a Muslim and they wanted to torture me with it. Exhausted, I slid to the floor. "Imma kill all you honkies!" I yelled, then I blacked out.

I woke to the sound of the food slot closing and tried to reach it before it shut but I was too late. On my hands and knees, I lowered my head and noticed a brown paper bag on the floor. Ripping it open, I ate the sandwiches. When I finished, I sat with my back to the door, looking around. My vision was bleary but not to where I couldn't see the Bible laying on the floor across the room. I sat for a minute, trying to figure out how to get rid of it. It wasn't supposed to be there in the first place!

I tried yelling, kicking and cursing out the officer but that got me nowhere. I'd have to outsmart him. Later, when he brought another bag, asking if he'd leave the food slot open so I could toss the Bible out. "No, I won't," he said, dropping the bag on the floor and slamming the food slot closed. Some days I didn't know if I was coming or going, if it was night or day. I had no way of telling, There were no windows.

After a few days in the observation cell, Dr. Darrin came to see me. He was in his early sixties, bald and wore rimless glasses. That's all I was able to see of him through the small food slot. "Hi, Anthony," he said with a smile. I stared at him from across the room. Then he started talking about forgiveness. I remember his words as if it were yesterday. He said, "You have to forgive them, Anthony, every one of them, including yourself." His words caught me off guard because I thought he'd dame to try and trick me into taking psyche medications. "It's going to be hard, and the hardest one to forgive will be yourself. You've known pain, heartache, failure and disappointment. You've known suffering from them but I'm here to tell you what you can do about them."

"This is one crazy dude," I thought. Still, something told me this guy was different. He kept at it, telling me about his God and salvation through His Son, Jesus Christ. Told me if I gave my life to Jesus, I would be saved from sickness, sin and even death. I tried arguing the case for Allah and Islam, but as with other Christians I'd encountered, he refused to be rattled. We went on like this for weeks. He presented his case for Jesus and I present mine for Allah. Every time Dr. Darrin came to see me, he said I reminded him of the apostle Paul, that we were so much alike. I'd always ask, "Who is Paul?" and his response was always the same – "Pick up that Bible, turn to the book of Acts and find out for yourself."

I was sitting in my cell one day, wondering why Dr. Darrin hadn't come to see me in over a week. I started to ask the officer but I didn't because I didn't want him to think I needed anything from him. A few more days passed and still no Dr. Darrin, which I found unusual because he'd normally see me at least three times a week. Finally, I asked the officer what was going on. "You haven't heard?" he asked. "Haven't heard what?" I said. "He died eight days ago.

Hearing that saddened and confused me. I was saddened because he died and I was confused as to how the death of a white man could make me sad. I walked over to the corner of my cell, sat down, and cried.

CHAPTER 17: THERE'S A MAN GOING 'ROUND...

"I say unto you, that likewise joy shall be in heaven
over one sinner that repenteth, more than over ninety and nine
just persons, which need no repentence." – Luke 15:7

Cancer was eating my body, the sickness of my sin, my soul. "I don't want to die like this," I thought. "Read the book," a voice said. It was a soft voice but it shook me to fear, more fear than I'd ever known. I realized at that moment I'd come face to face with the reality of God. Still, I asked, "Who are you?" "Read the book," it said again. I picked up the Bible. I didn't know where to start reading and was afraid to ask the voice so I opened it and began reading it on whatever page I had landed on. Paul asked, "Who are thou, Lord?" and He said, "I am Jesus whom thou persecuted."

The voice belonged to Jesus and I knew I was on my way to hell, if Jesus was anything like Allah. As a Muslim, I preached that God would do to those who disobeyed Him. He wasn't very forgiving. I sat there silent, not knowing what to do and after a while I wondered, "What happened to Paul?"

I went on reading: "But rise, and stand upon thy feet: for I have appeared unto thee for this purpose, to make thee a minister and a witness both of these things which thou hast seen, and of those things in which I will appear unto thee; Delivering thee from the people, and from the Gentiles, unto whom I now send thee. To open their eyes, and to turn them from darkness to light, and from the power of Satan unto

God, that they may receive forgiveness of sins, and inheritance among them which are sanctified by faith that is in me."

I sat the Bible down, not believe what I'd just read. Jesus didn't condemn Paul like I would have expected Him to, but instead said He would use Paul to reach out and help others. I sat thinking about that, how much different Jesus was from Allah. Jesus was forgiving but Allah would cast you into the lake of fire at the drop of a dime. I flipped the pages back to the beginning of the book of Acts and after I finished reading it, in its entirety, I could see why Dr. Darrin always said I reminded him of the apostle Paul. I again flipped the pages back, this time to the book of John. But I didn't get very far, only to Chapter three, verses 17 and 18: "For God sent not His Son into the world to condemn the world; but that the world through Him might be saved. He that believeth in Him is not condemned: but him that believeth…"

That's as far as I got. I couldn't read another word. I knew if I died at that moment, I'd be condemned because I lived a life of sin and hatred. The life I lived was one of pain and heartache, nothing I tried worked for me; my best thinking let me to a Suicide Observation cell where I was dying of cancer.

When I was a kid, I heard the old people say that they were "sick and tired of being sick and tired," and it wasn't until that day that I understood what they really meant. Sick and tired of being sick and tired, I bowed my head in prayer.

"Lord, I don't know where to start. I am scared. I've done so much wrong in my life. I've hurt so many people. I don't deserve anything good from you, as I've done nothing good in my life. But I am asking you to come into my life this very moment because I am hurting and in so much pain. The doctors can't help me. Lord, I'm dying."

EPILOGUE

Faith is something that can't be mentally produced. It comes by the way of trusting in the Lord, regardless of the circumstances we're faced with. It took faith in God for me to believe I was going to live when the doctors said I was going to die. They told me that during the later stages of prostate cancer, and the honest to God truth is – there were many days that I felt like giving up. But I didn't. I held on my faith in the promises of God and today I live a blessed, cancer-free life in Christ.

It wasn't easy for me because Satan tried everything, used every trick in the book trying to destroy my faith in the Lord. Living the life of a Christian isn't an easy thing to do. We'll have hard times and be challenged by Satan at every turn. There were moments in my life when the only thing I had to hold onto was faith, even though I couldn't feel it or see God's hand in my affairs.

So many people said to me, "Anthony, the Lord has a plan for you." They were right, He does. Within two years of incarceration, I joined the Black Muslim Movement and was indoctrinated with an extremely hate-filled belief. I was taught that my black life was important and the white life wasn't. They told me God was a black man and since I was made in His "image and likeness," I was superior to whites. I was taught to speak against them and their "white devil god," to beat, stab, starve and even kill them at every opportunity. I've done these things while claiming to be a servant of God. I'd claimed to love and fear God, all the while doing the bidding of Satan, who's given me nothing but hell all the days of my life. It was believing in such a hate-filled doctrine that eventually led me to attempt suicide.

Every trial, tribulation and every ounce of pain I suffered was designed and allowed so that I would eventually come fact to faith with Jesus. I have bee baptized by the Lord a Christian and by His authority, put a stop to the lawlessness and bad ways of the people.

Mark 16:15-18 says, "Go ye into all the world, and preach the Gospel to every creature. He that believeth and is baptized shall be saved; but he that believeth shall not be damned. And these signs shall follow them that believe; In My name shall they cast out devils; they shall speak with new tongues; they shall take up serpents; and if they drink any deadly thing, it shall not hurt them; they shall lay hands on the sick, and they shall recover."

There were so many times in my life when something really bad happened to me but I made it through it, telling myself afterwards that I was lucky. When I was shot three times in my chest and survived, I said, "Boy, I was lucky!" After flying through the windshield of a car going over a hundred miles per hour, landing 40 feet away, I said, "Boy, I was lucky!"

But luck had nothing to do with it, my friend. It was by God's grace. That's the reason I survived, that I'm alive today. By the grace of God.

I'd chose the path of trusting myself, looking at the world with a sense of entitlement, only to find the world didn't care and would give nothing back. This world offers us nothing but demons swarming the gates that hold us in sin. But the beauty in our condition is that it only takes a small candle to show us the way. God wants to help us and He's there with you now, wherever you are.

I've learned from my own experience that God is ready to bend the laws of physics to save me. I now put all my trust and faith in Him, no longer leaning on my own understanding. I've messed up my life so many times when I used my own mind to evaluate situations around me. After decades of struggle, poverty, prison and loneliness, I've relinquished all decision making authority that I have to God. Today, I have new friends in Christ, yet even they are human. I trust only God.

When I was diagnosed with prostate cancer, I suffered such physical, mental and spiritual pain. During the time when the pain was at its worst, Satan was very aggressive. He used the fear of me dying, fear of the sight of my own blood in my feces, my rapid weight loss and the fear of the medication I'd stopped taking that would cause me to die. I could go on and on. But even when I rebuked him in the name of Jesus, he tried to make me feel guilty about not being worried.

One of Satan's most successful tools is the sin of worrying and he's used this on me more times than I can count. For the better part of my life, Satan has over and over told me whatever situation I found myself in, it was hopeless. As a result, I found myself becoming fearful and worried about every little thing. Looking back at it all, me worrying was the avenue that most of my pain and suffering came from. If only I had trusted the Lord.

My past pains, aches, failures and disappointments wouldn't let me be, and just as Dr. Darrin said, I'd known my who life what it meant to suffer from them, but not what to do about them. I used to think they would miraculously disappear but they didn't. It took time. Without Christ, I was unable to put these things behind me. I held onto them until they became the only reality I knew. I became frozen with fear, so depressed to the point that I didn't want to live anymore.

Hebrews 8:12 says, "For I will be merciful to their unrighteousness and their sins and iniquities will I remember no more." The Lord says He's forgiven us our past failures so why do we hold onto them? Every morning God's mercy is new. Every morning I waked up and I see a new face. When I walk out of the housing unit, I see a new world. How did I get to this point? Forgiveness! I forgave everyone including myself. Over the years, I was able to forgive everyone who ever harmed or offended me in any way. And I won't lie and say it was an easy thing to do because it wasn't. It took time and a whole lot of praying, but I discovered my forgiveness had to be based on my faith and not my feelings.

CONTACT INFORMATION

Anthony B. Cook is an inmate presently incarcerated at Southeast Correctional Center in Charleston Missouri. He enjoys studying the Bible and writing and plans to take God's Word to our incarcerated youth in his hometown of St. Louis, Missouri when he is released in 2022. If you'd like to contact Anthony, you can do so by writing him at the following address: Anthony B. Cook #163116, 300 East Pedro Simmons Drive, Charleston, MO 63834 or email him at www.JPay.com.

Made in the USA
Monee, IL
17 August 2020